SELF-SUPERVISION

SELF-SUPERVISION

A Primer for Counselors and Helping Professionals

Patrick J. Morrissette, Ph.D., RMFT, NCC

Associate Professor

School of Health Studies

Brandon University

Routledge
Taylor & Francis Group
New York   London

Routledge is an imprint of the
Taylor & Francis Group, an informa business

Routledge Mental Health
Taylor & Francis Group
270 Madison Avenue
New York, NY 10016

Published in Great Britain by
Routledge Mental Health
Taylor & Francis Group
2 Park Square
Milton Park, Abingdon
Oxon OX14 4RN

© 2001 by Taylor & Francis Group, LLC
Routledge Mental Health is an imprint of Taylor & Francis Group

Printed in the United States of America on acid-free paper
10 9 8 7 6 5 4 3 2
International Standard Book Number-13: 978-1-58391-075-7
Cover design by Ellen Seguin
Printed by Edwards Brothers

Library of Congress Cataloging-in-Publication Data

Morrissette, Patrick J.
  Self-supervision : a primer for counselors and helping professionals / Patrick J. Morrissette.
     p. cm.
  Includes bibliographical references and index.
  ISBN 1-58391-075-1 (alk. paper)
    1. Counselors—Supervision on. 2. Psychotherapists—Supervision of. I. Title.
BF637.C6 M6225   2001
158'3—dc21
                                                            2001037801

Visit the Taylor & Francis Web site at
http://www.taylorandfrancis.com

and the Routledge Web site at
http://www.routledge.com

DEDICATION

This book is dedicated to the four most important,
loyal, and influential people in my life:
my lovely wife and best friend Debbie and
our three beautiful pearls Matthew, Alana, and Sam.

CONTENTS

Person-of-the-Counselor 56

Reflectivity: The Essence of Self-Supervision 77

Self-Supervision in Action 109

ACKNOWLEDGMENTS

I am very grateful to Professor John English from Brandon University's School of Health Studies for his support and encouragement throughout this project. John is a humble and unselfish man who freely shares his wealth of knowledge and experience. Even during brief hallway chats, he has a knack for creating an ambiance for reflection and growth. His creative nature and tenacity for seeking opportunities for personal growth is indeed contagious.

My writing was spurred by a spirit of scholarship that was fostered by Dr. Linda Ross, Dean of the School of Health Studies at Brandon University. Linda consistently supports the pursuit of scholarship and possesses the wonderful gift of "seeing the bigger picture." She is a kind and compassionate leader who listens carefully to the dreams of her colleagues and works toward helping others achieve their goals.

While preparing this book I often thought of my friend and mentor, Dean Ernie Rose from State University of New York at Binghamton. I had the pleasure of working with Ernie when he was Dean of Education and Human Services at Montana State University—Billings. Ernie promoted scholarly activity with tremendous enthusiasm and always found time to read, edit, and comment on various writing projects. Regardless of the size or significance of a project, Ernie consistently demonstrated a genuine interest in the interests and work of others.

I would also like to extend a very special thanks to Dr. Cheryl Storm, Professor of Marriage and Family Therapy at Pacific Lutheran University, who kindly agreed to review, offer editorial suggestions on, and prepare a forward to this book. Over the years, as a highly respected author and editor, Cheryl has supported innovation in systemic supervision and has encouraged conversation regarding self-supervision.

FOREWORD

Imagine that you are watching a therapist interview a family. You notice that the therapist seems a bit hesitant, pausing a little longer than normal before asking a question or reflecting on what was said. The therapist seems to be a little surprised, even concerned, by the clients' responses. There is a feeling of tension mounting in the therapeutic relationship. You begin to consider alternative therapeutic responses. Should the clients be asked to expand on what has been said so the therapist can better understand the situation, before sharing personal responses? Should the clients be directed to talk more about the issue with each other? Should the therapist openly comment on the tension? Is there something about the situation being described that is triggering the worry and preventing the therapist from relating in a typical fashion to the clients? You begin to share your thoughts and reactions to these questions with the therapist. You are talking to yourself.

All therapists have found themselves in some version of the above scenario. Many novice therapists turn to their supervisors for guidance in these moments, hoping for some way of deciding what is the best course to take. Even so, novice therapists often complain that their supervision does not occur when they most need it.

For many experienced therapists, there are no supervisors to turn to and no time regularly carved out of their grueling schedules for this type of discussion. Wouldn't it be great if therapists had an all-knowing, invisible supervisor sitting next to them at all times who could help find the best answers to these dilemmas? This invisible supervisor could help therapists find the answer that accessed the best of their abilities.

The practice of self-supervision can become this invisible supervisor—a supervisor who therapists can always count on to be at their side and have their best interests at heart. As Patrick Morrissette notes later in this volume, the idea of self-supervision is not new. What is new, in my opinion, is that Patrick has written a book that engages the reader in a self-supervision process that clearly illustrates the steps one can take to conduct one's own self-supervision. Patrick presents his ideas for self-supervision in a way that pulls the reader into the process. Clinical vignettes that focus on everyday therapeutic experiences are generously sprinkled throughout the text. As I found reminders of myself in these vignettes, I excitedly read on to see what conclusions Patrick drew about the therapist's work and hastily compared them to the conclusions I have made about my own work. It was nearly impossible not to answer the questions that were proposed in the text to promote personal reflection. My personal issues surfaced as Patrick said they would; many were not new to me but had been transformed over the years and warranted rethinking. Once they were noted, reflecting on them happened inadvertently. I found myself unintentionally self-supervising.

After conveying a comprehensive review of the development of the idea of self-supervision that spans a variety of disciplines, Patrick shows how therapists can not only create more of these types of conversations with themselves, but also become more proficient at using them to self-supervise their therapy. According to Patrick, self-supervision is a process of self-discovery that can easily be embedded in any therapist's daily practice at any point in his or her career. Most of his suggestions are eminently doable—small steps such as asking clients for feedback. Other suggestions, such as creating genograms or personal timelines and reviewing video- or audiotapes, are more time intensive and require more commitment. But even these can be easily adapted to fit any practitioner's setting or schedule. Strategies are thoughtfully outlined to help therapists explore their personhood, be more reflective during and after sessions, and review their work. Patrick concludes with an interesting discussion of the personal cost of caring, ways to identify when our work is taking a personal toll, and self-care steps to take to counter occupational hazards.

So beware reader: If your experience is at all like mine, you will probably find yourself becoming your own invisible supervisor even if you had no intention of self-supervising. You will most likely apply the ideas to your work as you read and reflect on ways you can learn from a renewed look at your therapy. You may be reminded of personal interfaces that have recently been out of your awareness and thus ultimately participate in a more personal experience than you had bargained for. And, like me, you will probably find yourself unexpectedly enjoying the conversations you have with yourself and excited about the personal learning that derives from the process of self-supervising. You may even find that self-supervision becomes one of your ongoing strategies of self-care.

Cheryl Storm, Ph.D.
Professor and Supervisor
Marriage and Family Therapy Program
Pacific Lutheran University
Tacoma, Washington

LIST OF TABLES AND FIGURES

INTRODUCTION

There is currently a voluminous amount of information available pertaining to direct counselor education, supervision, and training. The same cannot be said for methods that counselors can independently use to enhance self-awareness and to self-monitor their professional development and practice. For example, a comprehensive literature review revealed that despite its recognized value, the process of self-supervision is only addressed in a cursory fashion and "has tended to lurk in the background" (Lowe, 2000, p. 511). Further, although issues such as transference and countertransference are commonly treated in the supervision literature, specific steps that can be taken to identify and address such issues remain nebulous, enigmatic, and operationally vague. The intention of this text is to begin to fill the resulting void.

Self-supervision is a unique process whereby counselors can reflect on intrapersonal, interpersonal, and clinical issues that influence their work. This process might prove useful for counselors who are attempting to understand how and when personal attitudes, feelings, and values influence the counseling process and guide their work. Despite the lack of attention rendered to this process, self-supervision has the potential to be a valuable tool in the advancement of counselor development. A benefit of increased counselor development can be improved clinical services to clients, their families, and communities.

In terms of client welfare and enhanced service delivery, two primary advantages of self-supervision include increased quality assurance and economics (Donnelly & Glaser, 1992). With clinicians more focused on their personal process and skills, it is likely that treatment will be of higher quality and, therefore, more productive. With a heightened focus on treatment outcome, it is essential that efforts be made to increase the possibility of clients reaching their specified outcome measures (Johnson, 1995). Toward this end, helping clinicians need to scrutinize their work and carefully consider their strengths, needs, and limitations.

From an economic perspective, self-supervision could be beneficial in that additional personnel are not required to perform traditional supervisory functions. A common reaction to the economic benefit of self-supervision is that this process cannot be a substitute for the traditional supervisor-supervisee format. In other words, self-supervision may have its merits as a supplement to conventional supervision, but having another person assume a metaposition and point out personal and clinical blind spots is essential for supervisee growth. Those who argue against self-supervision as an independent form of supervision contend that clinicians are incapable of transcending their work and recognizing idiosyncratic attitudes and behaviors.

Despite these criticisms, the inherent challenges of providing supervision to counselors in remote areas coupled with changes in the health care system have contributed to a reduction of supervisory personnel in both the private and public sector. This development is not a new concern. Various authors (e.g., D. Martin & Gazda, 1970; Yager, 1987) reported that counselors were working in settings that did not include regularly assigned supervisors. Notwithstanding this shortcoming, counselors were still expected to demonstrate competence and express professional autonomy. The lack of appropriately trained supervisors translated into a decrease in the availability of conventional supervision. Yager and Park (1986) commented:

> Despite documented need for continued professional updating, typical counselor *supervision* [italics in original] (beyond that received as part of a graduate training program) is more accurately labeled *administration* [italics in original]. Often, the counselor reports periodically to the *supervisor* [italics in original] to discuss the particulars of the job but not to discuss specific difficulties encountered with clients that might promote self-development. (p. 6)

Martin and Gazda (1970) advocated self-evaluation methods as a way of enabling counselors to assess their own efforts and to facilitate personal and professional growth.

To assist counselors in their professional development and to avoid unfortunate professional-client transgressions, innovative self-supervision models have been developed. Lewis (1991) addressed the intense and hostile monitoring practices of managed health care and health insurance and stated:

> It may seem too much to suggest that psychotherapists need to monitor their own work and that training in doing so needs to begin during residency training. Such is so, however, and has been so since psychotherapy became a formal discipline. Competent psychotherapists monitor their own work, sometimes adding supervision, consultation, or small-group activity. (p. 142)

Self-supervision can be valuable for clinicians who work in a myriad of contexts. The process of self-supervision might prove especially valuable to clinicians who practice in relative geographic isolation, where traditional supervision may not be readily available. These professionals are often left without face-to-face interaction with a supervisor. Further, in the absence of colleagues with whom to discuss ethical, professional, or clinical issues, counselors are left grappling with sensitive issues in isolation. Consequently, counselors have less clinical support and must rely more heavily on their own intuitiveness and fortitude.

An argument against a pure reliance on self-supervision is that regardless of one's location, clinicians can communicate with supervisors via the telephone, teleconference, electronic mail, and so on. This is a valid and important point. With technological advances, professionals may have more resources at their disposal. Whether clinicians elect to enter into a self-supervisory process or find other ways to reflect on their work, however, will be a personal choice. In addition, it remains questionable whether conventional supervision is the most effective method for all clinicians. The lack of research contrasting traditional and nontraditional forms of supervision leaves room for debate. Future investigators may pursue studies contrasting the role, merit, and outcome of traditional versus self-supervision. Identifying which professionals benefit from which form of supervision becomes an important issue. Such a study would be analogous to investigating which clients benefit from which model of counseling. Currently, it is generally assumed that all counselors require and benefit from supervision offered by individuals who are deemed expert. This grandiose assumption, however, persists without any empirical support.

It is not the intention of this book to suggest that self-supervision is a new process. It has been over 20 years since Meyer (1978) proclaimed:

> The concept of self-supervision via tapes is not novel nor untried. In fact, more than ten years ago a report of the committee establishing educational standards for secondary school counselors recommended opportunities for self-evaluation and self-understanding using such methods as self-analysis or audio-tapes and videotapes. (p. 97)

The report alluded to by Meyer was also noted by Altekruse and Brown (1969) and was commissioned by the Committee on Counselor Education Standards in the Preparation of Secondary School Counselors. This report concluded that opportunities for self-evaluation and for the development of deeper self-understanding should be available for counselor candidates.

The primary intention of this book is to consolidate and synthesize the extant self-supervision literature and to integrate related information pertaining to the counselor-client relationship, person-of-the-counselor, reflectivity, supervisor-student relationships, and counselor self-care. Information for this book has been drawn from a variety of disciplines including marriage and family therapy, speech and hearing pathology, counseling, education, nursing, and psychiatry. I sincerely hope that others will critique and advance this present work and contribute to a better understanding of self-supervision.

By no means are the suggestions presented in this text intended as a definitive approach to self-supervision. Only with time will counselors determine whether self-supervision is a process they find useful in augmenting or replacing traditional direct supervision. Being able to combine parts or all aspects of the self-supervision process (e.g., audio- and videotape review components, clinical notes, client feedback) into a working model that improves treatment takes time and experience. As this framework becomes further articulated, formal research will be needed to support the value of this promising dimension of supervision.

This book has been designed in a logical fashion to assist readers in following the development of self-supervision. Chapter 1 traces the evolution of self-supervision and establishes a foundation for the chapters that follow. As noted in this historical overview, although models of self-supervision have developed in relative isolation, individuals from various helping professions and different parts of the world have commented on the intrinsic value and potential of self-supervision. These individuals have made significant contributions in further understanding self-supervision to varying degrees. Also, as self-supervision has evolved, constructivist theory has been instrumental in prompting supervisor-supervisee collaboration, as well as supervisee empowerment and self-regulation. An additional value of tracing the evolution of self-supervision is the discovery of various instruments designed to assist helping professionals in measuring their skills. Communication specialists and cognitive-behavioral theorists have designed instruments that have proven useful and, perhaps, adaptable to other professions. In sum, there have been visionaries who dared to think outside the lines to advance counselor development strategies and improve clinical services.

Chapter 2 examines the dynamics of the counselor-client relationship. To do so, the reciprocity and mutuality of the counseling relationship is emphasized. This chapter invites readers to deconstruct the counseling relationship through a systemic lens. To enhance the therapeutic relationship, counselors are encouraged to consider their propensity for transgressing boundaries and hindering treatment.

The implications associated with counselor centrality and over-involvement are also addressed. A discussion follows regarding how counselors who assume central positions when working with clients can unknowingly contribute to a hostile therapeutic environment and unintended client-counselor conflict. This chapter provides information on the transitional points that occur during treatment wherein counselors are invited to become overinvolved or play a more marginal role in order for clients to reach their goals.

Finally, the contentious issue of professional self-disclosure is also addressed in the context of counselor overinvolvement. Information regarding a self-closure continuum and disclosure styles are reviewed.

Chapter 3 focuses on the person-of-the-counselor. This chapter builds on the extant literature that examines how counselors' past and current issues can impact their work with clients. To promote counselor growth and development, contemporary models that have been designed to support the personhood of counselors are described and reviewed. Particular attention is devoted to the work of Aponte and his colleagues in their efforts to bridge the personhood of counselors and clinical intervention. Although this issue sounds straightforward, scholars in this area have explored the less-than-obvious impact of family of origin and unresolved issues regarding service delivery. Available strategies that can be employed to assist counselors in exploring their personhood are examined, and include autobiographies, genograms, and timelines.

Chapter 4 emphasizes the need for critical reflectivity in self-supervision. In providing a historical sketch of the reflection process, this chapter begins to integrate the work of various scholars who have employed the reflective process to enhance their work. The development and use of critical thinking skills is encouraged to enhance higher order thinking, counselor development, and clinical service.

To provide a balanced view, important critiques presented by Ixer and Eraut are included. These authors considered the process, assessment, and practicality of reflection. Their treatises are extremely valuable in tempering an all-or-nothing approach to reflectivity. Based on these critical perspectives, a moderate stance is suggested and practitioners can independently determine the usefulness of reflection.

Underscored in this chapter is the courage and integrity involved in entering the reflective process. In addition to reflecting on the significance of past events, the importance of connecting information with one's current interactions with clients is highlighted. Important questions and guidelines for counselors are provided, based on the excellent work of various individuals.

Finally, the use of mentoring to introduce less experienced colleagues to reflectivity is reviewed. Although mentoring is a potentially valuable process, related issues of intimacy, conflict, dependency, and termination are discussed.

Chapter 5 delves into the actual practice of self-supervision. Along with discussing how counselors can gather and synthesize information from a variety of sources and time frames, this chapter elaborates on the guiding principles and pragmatics of self-supervision. Intrapersonal, interpersonal, and clinical aspects of an interview are reviewed to demonstrate how past and present issues can impact counselors and their relationships with clients. In addition to providing objectives and a rationale for each focus area, practical strategies are provided for counselor consideration.

Finally, Chapter 6 examines the historical trend to neglect work-related problems within the mental health professions, and the growing importance of counselor self-care. In addition to discussing counselor vulnerability, the association between counselor emotional well-being and service delivery is underlined. The exceptional work of Figley in the area of compassion fatigue and Pearlman and Saakvitne's investigation into counselor vicarious traumatization is given noteworthy attention. Other constructs pertaining to occupational hazards include burnout, stress, critical incident stress, and post-traumatic stress disorder. To assist counselors, several proactive strategies are explored and suggested.

Counselor Self-Supervision: A Historical Overview

*There are two main responses to a disturbing therapeutic experience and the likeli-
hood of unconscious contributions from the therapist: the insightful and open pursuit of self-supervision or the development of major resistances to that process.*

—Robert Langs, 1979

The term *self-supervision* appears to have surfaced concurrently in Europe
and North America during the late 1970s. According to Littrell, Lee-Borden,
and Lorenz (1979), publications and conference presentations pertaining
to counselor self-supervision were only beginning to emerge during this
period (e.g., Bandura, 1978; Kahn, 1976; Lecomte & Bernstein, 1978;
Meyer, 1978).

In 1979, the British psychoanalyst Robert Langs devoted a chapter in
his book, *The Supervisory Experience*, to self-supervision. By his own ad-
mission, Langs noted that the chapter was, in fact, only an afterthought.
To his knowledge, although the self-analytic process had been addressed
in the literature, no papers had been written specifically on the subject of
self-supervision. As a result, Langs committed himself to articulating a
process whereby his students could examine their thoughts, feelings, and
actions in relation to their clients. Within this process, students were encouraged to increase their self-awareness and better understand relational
dynamics.

A year earlier, on the other side of the Atlantic, Meyer (1978) had published a review paper regarding self-supervision, and Lecomte and Bernstein (1978) had delivered an address to the annual meeting of the American Personnel and Guidance Association entitled "Development of Self-Supervision Skills Among Counselor Trainees." Meyer discussed how behavioral principles could be used to influence counselor self-control and self-management. He also remarked that the concept of self-supervision was not novel or untried. In his review of the literature, although the term self-supervision never surfaced, Meyer identified counselor self-management, self-control, self-analysis, self-monitoring, and self-evaluation programs.

In her article "The Irma Dream, Self-Analysis, and Self-Supervision," Blum (1995) described how, through the psychoanalytic method and process, Freud considered himself his own analyst and supervisor. According to Blum, Freud's self-analysis and self-supervision proceeded primarily in reference to dreams and focused on the concepts of transference and countertransference. Although the term self-supervision was being introduced to the counseling profession, clearly Sigmund Freud's interest in dream analysis and self-analysis was a precursor, and, instrumental in the eventual process of counselor self-exploration.

Similar to other historical developments in the helping professions, when charting the evolution of counselor self-supervision, it becomes clear that the emergence of self-supervision developed in relative isolation in different helping professions and in different parts of the world.

☐ Broadening the Supervisory Lens

Ultimately, Langs (1979) might be credited with developing the first model of counselor reflection and monitoring wherein the reciprocal nature of counseling was emphasized and examined. In contrast to Freud's self-analysis, Langs considered self-supervision to be broader than self-analysis and to have a much wider perspective because it was competency-based, identified and punctuated individual strengths, and continued even when counseling appeared to be going well. During this process, clinicians attempted to remain mindful of various intrapersonal, interpersonal, and larger systems issues that impinged on the counseling relationship and, ultimately, on the outcome of treatment. Self-supervision evolved into an ongoing search for therapeutic errors (Bross, 1982), countertransferences, and the identification of positive aspects of a counselor's work.

Langs (1979) contended that self-supervision was a disregarded dimension of supervision and further postulated that the lack of attention rendered to the self-supervision process was fueled by two major assumptions. First, it was assumed that counselors would remain vigilant to conscious and unconscious issues that were identified during formal supervision, continually scrutinize their work with clients, and incorporate supervisory attitudes that were learned in the traditional supervision context to resolve issues related to therapeutic impasse. In essence, this process would parallel the traditional two-person supervisory situation whereby "accrued insights would be maintained on some level as part of a self-examining process related to each therapeutic experience" (Langs, p. 384).

Second, it was assumed that counselors would use and transfer the same skills they used to supervise others to themselves. Under this assumption, counselors were expected to transcend their clinical work, assume a metaposition, become introspective, and consider the origin and impact of issues that impinged on counseling. Of course, it was presupposed that counselors were prepared and competent to execute this task without formal guidelines or mentoring. The aforementioned assumptions, coupled with the lack of discussion and investigation regarding the self-examining process, prompted Langs to conclude that the proposed theory was not being accurately translated into actual practice. A similar finding was later echoed by Casey, Smith, and Ulrich (1989), who also believed that the ability of students and clinicians to self-supervise did not happen by chance. These latter authors suggested that, "probably few persons perceive that they have totally reached this stage . . . that they do not need some kind of peer interaction for continued professional growth and development" (p. 52).

From a psychoanalytical perspective, Langs (1979) understood self-supervision to be a process whereby counselors would monitor their own inner experiences and the communications of clients for unconscious perceptions and commentaries on therapeutic endeavors. Although he articulated skills that he used with students to help them gain a better understanding of self, Langs believed that he made the same assumptions and failed to delineate the process and design a methodology.

From these two assumptions alone, one begins to sense the high degree of insight, rigor, and responsibility involved in deconstructing the counseling process to improve self-awareness, clinical skills, and quality service to clients. Despite sounding straightforward and reasonable in theory, however, the skills and demands inherent in the self-supervision process remain vague and enigmatic and cannot be underestimated. Langs (1979) expressed concern about the lack of attention to counselor self-examination and wrote:

> Viewed in the worst light, the lack of literature on the subject might be taken as evidence of a considerable degree of neglect, disinterest, and fear of self-supervision, not only in terms of formal investigations, but also in respect to actual practice. (p. 386)

He continued:

> For too long now we have taken self-supervision for granted, neglecting the development of a basic format and failing to attend to the very specific problems involved. As with every other dimension of the therapeutic experience, self-supervision can rely only minimally on the therapist's natural proclivities and basic understanding; much must be done to sharpen these assets and to bring them into full awareness so that they might serve as efficacious therapeutic tools. (p. 299)

In directly addressing his concern, Langs (1979) suggested a model and format for self-supervision. Within his proposed model, Langs encouraged counselors to obliterate memories of past sessions, knowledge, and attitudes. This process is comparable to the bracketing procedures found in qualitative inquiry whereby researchers attempt to suspend assumptions and biases so that they can be open to different perspectives and shared narratives. Langs was interested in having counselors foster a new beginning during each session with clients and search for the unknown. Succinctly stated, this process created a state of mind in which

> old concepts can be discovered anew, and revised as needed, and new self-supervisory issues can best be detected, while old ones are remembered in a specific context during the session. In all, this approach fosters the setting aside of relatively fixed self and general knowledge, in favor of the fresh discovery of truths about oneself, the patient, and the therapeutic process. (p. 386)

To accomplish this process, counselors suspend or interrupt the way in which they perceive, think about, and interact with clients. They attempt to transcend normal interactions and try to broaden their perspective by considering behaviors in unique ways. This generally involves generating different hypotheses and reformulating the problem behavior. As discussed later, however, not all counselors may be able to accomplish this rigorous task.

☐ The Influence of Constructivism

What is remarkable about Langs's (1979) vision is the eventual emergence and influence of constructivist and postmodern thought on counselor training and supervision (Franklin & Nurius, 1998; McNamee & Gergen, 1995; Sexton & Griffin, 1997). In concrete terms, there was a movement toward counselors turning in on themselves and looking inward for a better understanding of self in relation to others. As Mahoney (1991) remarked,

Whether our interest lies more with psychological change or stabilization, it involves an inevitable amplification of self-study. Although psychological self-focus may not be universal, it has clearly become one of the cardinal characteristics of the twentieth-century humanity. Living in the most complex and changing environment in Earth's history, we humans have exhibited a growing fascination with ourselves, our self-awareness, and an awareness of our awareness. (p. 6)

As a result of this movement in counseling, no longer were counselor thoughts, feelings, and behaviors considered separate from the professional-client relationship. Rather, working toward understanding how a counselor's disposition and context could influence transactions with clients introduced an expanded and critical dimension to supervision.

During this developmental period, a less objective and more humanistic/existential perspective on human interactions was evidenced. Bandura (1978) succinctly asserted that, " People are not only perceivers, knowers, and actors. They are also self-reactors with capacities for reflective self-awareness that are generally neglected in information-processing theories based on computer models of human functioning" (p. 356). Along these lines, Neufeldt (1997) commented that in a reflective stance counselors could examine their actions, emotions, and thoughts, as well as the interactions between themselves and clients in a profound and meaningful way. In defending personal reflection, Mahoney (1991) contended that this process was not an antiseptic expression of logic but rather, "an active, exploratory, self-examining attitude that embodies a passionate commitment to knowing" (p. 25). To him it was a continual integration of thinking, feeling, and actions.

The notion of *reflexivity* can be understood as a bending back on itself (Steier, 1991) or a turning back of one's experience upon oneself (Mead, 1962). Embedded in the concept of reflexivity is a circular process wherein counselors focus on issues of self-reference and how these issues can influence their perceptions and interactions with clients. The concept of reflexivity directly challenges the traditional idea of counselor objectivity and emphasizes the idea that what counselors say about clients is merely a reflection of something about themselves (e.g., values). In sum, with the emergence of constructivism, counselors were invited to consider how their private and personal ideas and life experiences influenced their knowing process and interpersonal relationships.

As discussed throughout this book, self-supervision is a continual process that concerns both the strengths and needs of counselors. It is not a process that occurs occasionally with a simple focus on either counselor needs or weaknesses but rather a process that embraces a holistic perspective. For example, when queried about how they reflect on their work, counselors report a tendency to review their work after disappointing sessions, when conflictual interactions with clients surface, or when clinical goals are not being achieved. It is as if an alarm suddenly sounds prompting counselors to investigate the therapeutic process. For these professionals, the reflection process does not occur on an ongoing basis and is usually provoked by negative factors. Conversely, counselors who enter into the self-supervision process are interested in tracking moment by moment transactions with clients to better understand personal issues that affect their interactions with clients and counseling in general. In concrete terms, self-supervision should be understood as an underlying philosophy and not a technique or strategy.

☐ A Changing Tide: The Influence of a Solution-Focused Orientation

Historically, counselor supervision has been steeped in a problem-focused orientation and students have been conditioned to focus on negative aspects of an interview. In retrospect, it is no wonder that students have traditionally dreaded the infamous supervision hour and have walked away feeling defeated and insecure about their skills and ability to help clients. Unfortunately, for many students, clinical supervision does not represent a time of support and encouragement. Rather, supervision is associated with the involvement of *expert* supervisors who point out mistakes and suggest more effective ways of conducting treatment and helping clients. As noted by Neufeldt (1997), "Expert authorities transmit knowledge to uninformed counselors, in what Freire (1993) has called the banking concept of education, in which, in this case, supervisees are receptacles and supervisors make deposits" (p. 193). This process serves to perpetuate the obvious supervisor-counselor hierarchy (top-down), inadvertently disempowers counselors, and places unnecessary pressure on supervisors to appear wise and omnipotent about all types of clients and cultures.

When considering traditional supervision practices, two major issues surface: student counselor disempowerment and supervisor development and skills. In terms of the former issue, there may be residual effects for clients when counselors are second-guessed or criticized by supervisors. For instance, counselors whose efforts are criticized may inadvertently begin criticizing client efforts in a parallel fashion. These counselors may believe that their supervisors consider their efforts to be substandard and, in turn, accuse clients of poor effort.

Over the years, there has been a persistent and erroneous assumption that effective counselors are also competent supervisors. Although the

American Association for Marriage and Family Therapy has long recognized the specialized Approved Supervisor designation, only recently has the National Board of Certified Counselors developed the Clinical Approved Supervisor designation. The primary purpose of such designations is to emphasize that supervision is a specialty area requiring specific education and training. It should not be assumed that professionals who possess theoretical knowledge and impressive clinical skills can translate this information and ability to others in a supervisory context. Approved supervisor designations have been created to demonstrate that clinical supervision is a complex enterprise that demands specialized training.

The influence of constructivist philosophy and the emergence of competency-based supervision and, eventually, solution-oriented supervision has been important to the ongoing evolution of self-supervision.

☐ Competency-Based to Solution-Oriented Supervision

Although the counselor supervision literature refers to competency-based practices, this term is somewhat misleading. In short, students were essentially expected to select segments of their audio- or videotaped interviews for supervisor and peer review. Although this process recognized the abilities of students and served to elevate their status within the supervision relationship, supervisors remained in a superior, directing role. It appears that student competency was defined very narrowly. Despite this criticism, the development of competency-based supervision was nevertheless an important step in the evolution of self-supervision.

Over time, what has become obvious is the gradual movement from a supervisor-directed experience to a student-initiated process, and eventually to an independent learning experience. Inherent in this shift is that hierarchical supervisor-student relationships have been compressed, power imbalances have been reduced, and there has been increased confidence in counselors' ability to identify their own needs and to monitor their own learning. Within the context of contemporary solution-focused supervision, for instance, counselors are viewed as competent colleagues (Thomas, 1994).

Clearly, there are obvious similarities between solution-focused supervision and solution-focused counseling. In other words, just as counselors work diligently to assist clients to uncover strengths and competencies, supervisors invite counselors into a similar process. According to Juhnke (1996), solution-focused supervision emphasizes competence, strengths, and possibilities rather than deficits, weaknesses, and limitations. To counter student tendencies to highlight their mistakes and shortcomings, solution-focused supervisors help counselors identify and amplify even the smallest treatment success.

Another advancement toward counselor self-supervision includes *Sharevision.* Fontes (1995) described this innovative approach and explained how it was based on constructivist principles. Sharevision was designed and implemented as an adjunct to more traditional supervision or as a replacement for it. This form of collaborative supervision empowers counselors while enhancing cohesion and mutual support. Realizing that traditional supervision that was poorly executed could effectively contribute to a counselor's diminished sense of adequacy, Sharevision countered this trend by focusing on counselor strengths and personal power.

Still, today it is not unusual for counselors to present cases to their supervisors that appear to be going poorly. Rarely will counselors present a case where their skills are obvious or when client progress is evident. In the former scenario, counselors seem programmed to focus on problems, obstacles, and perceived shortcomings. As one student recently remarked, "I have just been conditioned to speak about the mistakes I make." In describing a major drawback to a problem-focused approach to supervision, Wetchler (1990) contended:

> If supervision takes on a problem-resolution stance to trainee development, the focus will be on supervisee mistakes. This focus will highlight things that supervisees do wrong rather than what they do correctly. A problem orientation serves to reinforce supervisees' feelings of inadequacy as they attend to mistakes, which further supports feelings of confusion. A continuous focus on problems can lead to feelings of therapeutic inadequacy as supervisees begin to define themselves as *trainees who make mistakes* [italics in original] rather than *clinicians who have successes* [italics in original]. (p. 131)

Over time, several models of counselor self-introspection have been influential in what has come to be called self-supervision. Despite the differences among these models, what remains consistent is a focus on enhanced counselor self-awareness and skill development.

☐ Methods of Self-Introspection

There are several methods that describe processes whereby students and clinicians in the helping professions reflect on their clinical interactions with clients. Examples include interpersonal process recall (Kagan, 1980), self-critique (Bernstein & Lecomte, 1979), self-management (Hector, Elson, & Yager, 1977; Kahn, 1976), self-analysis (Altekruse & Brown, 1969), self-generated performance feedback (Robinson, Kurpius, Froehle, 1979), self-monitoring (Haferkamp, 1989), self-instruction (Cormier & Cormier, 1976; Robinson & Kinnier, 1988), and self-evaluation (Fuhrmann, 1978; Martin & Gazda, 1970). Each method is briefly described below to provide readers with a historical sketch and an opportunity to contrast commonalities and differences.

Interpersonal Process Recall

Interpersonal Process Recall (IPR) was discovered and developed by Kagan (1980) and has been used with a variety of helping professionals. Kagan developed this process to provide helping professionals with opportunities to see themselves in action through the use of videotape.

As reported in Kagan (1980), Kagan and his colleagues had observed in 1962 that

> stimulated recall by means of videotape could enable people to understand themselves better, to recognize their impact on others and to realize the impact others have on them and could allow people an unusual opportunity to try out new interpersonal modes of relating and responding." (p. x)

The fundamental purpose of IPR is to assist helpers in becoming better listeners and more effective communicators. Although admitting that his process of videotaping and reviewing interpersonal interactions occurred serendipitously, Kagan's efforts were at the forefront in the use of technology with counselor training.

IPR is directed at developing three general sets of skills, including the ability to (a) clearly understand what a person is saying both overtly and covertly and on both the cognitive and affective levels, (b) recognize and label the impact another person is having on us, and (c) share with people what is heard and our internal reactions.

A desired outcome of IPR is that professionals become more aware of personal and client lifestyles, behavior, and attitudes. It is assumed that as clinicians demonstrate an increased interest and learn more about clients, clients will in turn notice this interest and respond with increased self-disclosure. The overall goal is to develop relationships with clients that are more deeply involved and meaningful (Kagan, 1980).

A perceived strength of the IPR model is that participants are viewed as "the best authority on their own dynamics and the best interpreter of their own experience" (Neufeldt, 1997, p. 194). Kagan's work is significant in relation to self-supervision in that counselors are given credit for noticing and understanding elements of an interaction to which they alone are privy.

Self-Critique

According to Bernstein and Lecomte (1979), the three principle components of self-critique training include (a) a student's initial self-evaluation, (b) a student's rationale for selecting a videotaped excerpt for review, and (c) a comparison of a student's self-evaluation with that of his
or her peers in a supervision group. In addition to outlining the process of
student learning, Bernstein and Lecomte provided excellent questions,
described in Table 1.1.

As Bernstein and Lecomte (1979) pointed out, the self-critique technique "stresses counselor self-evaluation based upon focused self-obser-
vation" (p. 73). It appears that the focus of this technique is placed on the
clinical aspect of interviews and not necessarily on the mutuality between
students and clients.

Self-Management

Kahn (1976) remarked that the concept of self-management was not a
novel idea and could be traced back to the Socratic dictum, "Know thyself." He explained how the term self-management falls under terms such
as self-control, self-discipline, self-regulation, and self-help. According to
Bradley (1989), self-management techniques were evident throughout
the behavioral supervision methodology and were operationally defined
as "the ability of individuals to make personal behavioral adjustment decisions and actions based on analyses of self and the environment" (p.
169). The four basic components of self-management include (a) self-
monitoring, (b) self-measurement, (c) self-mediation, and (d) self-maintenance (Kahn, 1976). Self-monitoring involves observing one's own

---

TABLE 1.1. Potential Self-Critique Questions

1. What were my alternatives to say or do at this point?
2. What was I hearing my client say and/or observing my client do?
3. What was I thinking about my observations?
4. How did I choose from among the alternatives?
5. How did I intend to proceed with my selected responses?
6. What did I actually say or do?
7. What effect(s) did my response have on my client?
8. How, then, would I evaluate the effectiveness of my response?
9. What would I do differently now?

Bernstein and Lecomte, copyright 1979 in *Counselor Education and
Supervision.* Reprinted with permission of Pearson Education
Publication

behavior. The purpose of this process is to increase self-awareness and self-understanding. To accomplish this, counselors reflect on the consequences of their thinking, feeling, and behavioral patterns. More specifically, effort is made to determine how, when, and from where certain thoughts, feelings, and behaviors emanate.

Self-measurement assesses the extent of counselor difficulty. In order to measure the problem and to determine what level of intervention is required, counting or timing of specific behaviors (e.g., verbal comments) occurs. Self-mediation involves developing and implementing strategies to alter self-selected problem behaviors. Finally, self-maintenance focuses on the continuous monitoring and measuring of the self-mediation program.

Kahn (1976) pointed to the personal responsibility factor as both the most therapeutically productive and the most limiting characteristic of this model. He noted that self-management required motivation. Further, to be effective, self-managers would need to be rational and perceptive in order to "monitor relevant feedback on his or her behavior, to objectively measure that behavior and creatively devise and maintain strategies that will change that behavior" (p. 179). In addition, to avoid frustration and failure, self-managers would have to be aware of the variables influencing the behavior to be managed and have some control over the manipulation of these variables.

Self-Analysis

In an effort to better understand the effectiveness of self-analysis in the development of counseling skills, Altekruse and Brown (1969) embarked on a study to provide preliminary research data. These authors attempted to determine whether structured self-analysis of counselor candidate tape recordings could assist them in changing their counseling behavior. The study involved an experimental and a control group. The experimental group had access to the Counselor Self-Interaction Analysis (CSIA). The CSIA was a method of analyzing their counseling tape recordings and was a modification of analysis instruments. The self-analysis process involved students reviewing their own tape recordings of interviews and categorizing their responses in accordance with the CSIA system. More specifically, a counselor could "determine whether he or the client dominated the counseling session, how many direct responses vs. indirect responses he used, the type of responses he used most often, and the type of responses he made following specific counselee responses" (p. 109). This study concluded that, "Results of an external analysis of pre- and post-counseling tape recordings indicated that while most students moved toward the use of more indirective responses, the group which used self-analysis changed significantly more" (p. 112). Although their initial findings were promising, these authors were uncertain whether students who used the instrument would continue to demonstrate behavior change or if the instrument would be useful to practicing counselors.

Self-Generated Performance Feedback

Robinson, Kurpius, and Froehle (1979) explored the concept of counselor self-generated performance feedback based on self-evaluation/instruction. This form of self-evaluation/feedback involved "participants responding to a video-taped client and then orally evaluating their own response on the basis of a performance standard" (p. 91).

To investigate novice counselor response leads, these authors conducted a study that examined the effect of self-generated performance feedback, of expert feedback, and of no performance feedback. Based on the results of their study, these authors found that "participants who generated their own feedback reported a high level of satisfaction with this approach to learning a basic skill. They reported that they received the desired feedback without undue anxiety over mistakes because they were their own feedback agents" (p. 98). According to these authors, participants appreciated the opportunity to design and monitor their own actions without continuous surveillance. A reported strength of self-generated performance feedback is that counselors can embark on skill development without direct supervision.

Self-Monitoring

The process of self-monitoring in counseling has been affiliated with self-supervision. Several authors (Haferkamp, 1989; Lewis, 1979, 1991; Matthews & Marshall, 1988; Williams, 1995) have addressed the development of self-monitoring skills. In an attempt to connect research with practice, Haferkamp provided a review of the literature on self-monitoring and discussed its implications for counseling relationships. Within her overview, she surveyed various studies that examined the social behaviors and practices (e.g., self-disclosure) among low and high self-monitors. Although not specifically addressing self-monitoring among counselors, her efforts can be viewed as a first step that provides valuable information for counselor educators, supervisors, and students. In discussing the relevance of self-disclosure to counseling, Haferkamp hypothesized that "self-monitoring describes individual differences in person's abilities to adapt to their behaviors in interpersonal contexts. Finally, self-monitoring has pervasive effects on attitudes, attributions, expectancies and other social cognitions; all of these are constructs of vital concern to counselors and social-psychologists alike" (p. 291). Because Haferkamp set out to survey the literature and report on findings that could enhance the work of counselors, she did not discuss the actual self-monitoring process.

In contrasting high self-monitors and low self-monitors, Snyder (1979) portrayed high self-monitors as proficient in modifying their behavior to fit a particular context. According to Snyder, they seem to ask, "What does this situation want me to be and how can I be that person?" On the other hand, low self-monitors were described as more self-oriented and ask, "Who am I and how can I be me in this situation?" Results from a study conducted by Matthews and Marshall (1988) suggested that low self-monitors tend to assume a uniform therapeutic approach. In contrast, high self-monitors "may be less concerned with fitting a presenting clinical problem into a theoretical framework than with finding an intervention that fits the specific problem or client" (p. 434).

It appears that there are implications for counseling depending on which category professionals fall within. In the former scenario, counselors may be more sensitive to contextual cues and thus search for a theoretical and interpersonal fit between themselves and clients. Such counselors may be more flexible and use an eclectic approach.

Self-Instruction

Robinson and Kinnier (1988) described self-instructional training (SI) as a process consisting of a videotape that demonstrated counselor tacting response leads (CTRLs), vignettes depicting appropriate CTRLs, self-generated performance feedback vignettes, and assessment vignettes. Counselors were given a limited time to respond to a vignette. Results from their training program suggested that SI can be as effective as traditional classroom training for teaching paraphrasing and formulating CTRLs. These authors did note that SI programs are probably better suited "for graduate students who are mature and perhaps prefer self-guided learning" (p. 145).

Self-Evaluation

D. Martin and Gazda (1970) described a method whereby counselors could monitor their work through self-evaluation. This process involved using four psychotherapeutic interaction scales to assess their work: Non-Possessive Warmth (NPW), Accurate Empathy (AE), Intensity and Intimacy of Interpersonal Contact (IIC), and Therapist's Genuineness or Self-

Congruence (GEN). The study involved two groups of counselors, one that evaluated their own counseling immediately following each counseling session and one that did not self-evaluate. The self-evaluations were later reviewed by a supervisor. Results of Martin and Gazda's study, contrasting these two groups, indicated that while "counselors in this study who used these scales for self-evaluation did make significant gains in their ability to offer high therapeutic conditions, their gains were significantly greater on only one of the four scales when compared with counselors who received traditional counseling practicum training" (p. 91). Counselors who used the scales for self-evaluation demonstrated greater gains in their ability to provide higher levels of AE. Based on their findings, these authors suggested that the self-evaluation method might prove beneficial for counselors who could not obtain field supervision. It was conceded, however, that the effect of the absence of the counselor-supervisor relationship was unknown.

Fuhrmann (1978) proposed a method for self-evaluation and for generating steps toward enhanced counseling skills independent of supervisors. She believed that her approach provided counselors with an open, adaptable, and reliable approach that encouraged practitioners to capitalize on their gut-level feelings. This method consisted of counselors rating themselves on a continnuum following an interview. The contiuum ranged from 0 (terrible) to 8 (superb). Once they rated themselves, counselors asked themselves two basic questions: (a) What factors contributed to your rating this interview as high as you do? and (b) What would you have to do to make it a perfect interview? Fuhrmann emphasized the need for realistic counselor goals throughout the self-evaluation process. It was her experience that counselors who used this method gradually learned to trust their gut-level reactions and internalized a self-evaluation mechanism on which they could rely.

Up to this point it would appear that counselor educators have been the primary influence on the evolution of self-supervision. Although these practitioners and theoreticians are deserving of much credit, the pioneering work of communication specialists must be acknowledged. As described below, speech and hearing specialists have contributed greatly to the literature and have spearheaded the development of self-supervision evaluation instruments.

☐ Communication Specialists' Influence in the Development of Self-Supervision

Over the years, self-supervision has received increased attention and its value has been recognized in the allied helping professions. In fact, communication specialists have led the way in describing the self-supervision process and in developing evaluative instruments (e.g., Crago, 1987; Donnelly and Glaser, 1992; Dowling, 1979). This effort was substantiated by an entire published monograph entitled *Self-Supervision: A Career Tool for Audiologists and Speech-Language Pathologists*, prepared by the American Speech-Language-Hearing Association (ASHA; Casey, Smith, & Ulrich, 1989). Dowling remarked that self-supervision encompassed a variety of skills including accurate clinical diagnosis and the translation of the diagnostic results into a viable treatment program. She went on to say that "Skillful management should be followed by evaluation which includes an examination of therapy objectives and procedures, client behaviors and most importantly, your own behavior. What did you do that facilitated or impeded clinical progress?" (p. 37)

Crago (1987) believed that self-exploration entailed two processes: (a) looking inward at personal behaviors, processes, and interactions, and (b) changing behavior and moving ahead. She further elaborated, "Self-exploration implies both an inward, detailed, search and find process of analysis and an outward, pushing forward process of discovery into new uncharted ways of behaving" (p. 138). Crago contended that professionals who self-explore use themselves in meaningful and knowledgeable ways and that, "The ability to analyze one's functioning and determine a route for desired change is an essential skill for becoming and remaining a competent professional" (p. 138).

☐ Developmental Frameworks of Self-Supervision

The aforementioned monograph published by ASHA referred to a three-stage continuum of professional growth that included (a) an evaluation feedback stage, (b) a transitional stage, and (c) a self-supervision stage. Almost a decade earlier, Littrell, Lee-Borden, and Lorenz (1979) had proposed a four-stage developmental framework for counselor supervision. Comparable to the ASHA-endorsed continuum, Littrell et al. considered self-supervision to be the final stage. The four stages of counselor development proposed by these authors included (a) a relationship/goal setting/contract stage, (b) a counseling/therapeutic/teaching stage, (c) a consulting stage, and (d) a self-supervising stage. In describing their view of the self-supervision process, Littrell et al. wrote:

> The basic premise of self-supervision is that the principles of supervision are applied for self-development of clinical skills and professional growth. In other words, the concept, tasks, and competencies of clinical supervision are utilized for directing and assessing one's own performance. Specific, detailed, and objective observations are planned and implemented; result-

ing data are analyzed and interpreted; and results or conclusions are integrated in a plan for subsequent action. (p. 8)

In an attempt to describe the self-supervision stage, Casey et al. (1989) reported that clinicians hold themselves accountable for effectiveness and remain responsible for continued skill development and professional self-growth. According to these authors, clinicians who self-supervise independently analyze their clinical behavior and, based on their subsequent findings, plan and employ necessary changes. As Casey et al. pointed out, not all students or clinicians will achieve this level of independent functioning: "For some individuals, it remains an elusive goal even after many years of professional experience" (p. 10). Unfortunately, Casey et al. did not attempt to identify personal or professional variables that would contribute to one's ability or inability to effectively self-supervise. As noted later, however, the ability to become and remain vulnerable and appreciate personal contributions to the counseling process is considered central to self-supervision. Aponte (1994b), for example, believed that professional helpers could benefit from training that encouraged introspection and an appreciation of personal vulnerability. Of course, this process might be easier when cases appear to be going well. With cases in which clinical goals are not being achieved, however, self-scrutiny and personal accountability may not be free-flowing. To be more specific, when a clinical case appears to be floundering, clinicians are faced with the task of considering their contributions to be the problem.

☐ Self-Assessment Instruments

Casey et al. (1989) developed the "Clinician/Supervisee Skills Self-Assessment Instrument" to assist students and clinicians in the self-supervision process. The self-assessment instrument is a flexible tool that can be adjusted to suit the needs of individual counselors. The instrument identifies various *clinical tasks* and *competency levels*. In regards to the level of competency within each selected clinical task, clinicians ask themselves, "How important is this competency for effectiveness in my program?" In other words, clinicians begin to prioritize task importance in relation to the degree of importance a program attributes to a task area (e.g., allowing for equal talk time between partners). In terms of actual task competency, clinicians ask themselves, "How satisfied am I with my ability to perform this skill?" A strength of this instrument is that clinicians are encouraged to prioritize tasks within their given program, and thus they begin to focus on areas that require the most attention. This instrument may be particularly helpful to beginning clinicians who wish to narrow their focus and solidify skills in certain areas. Rather than working toward increasing skills in each area of their clinical work, clinicians assume a developmental approach and determine the most important skills. An obvious advantage of this approach is that beginning clinicians are less likely to become overwhelmed with interview/clinical tasks.

Case Vignette

As a first-year master's-level family therapy intern, John was instructed to follow the stages of the initial interview as outlined by Haley (1976). It was believed that encouraging John to follow specific stages to guide the interview process would lessen his anxiety and help him to gather important information in a sequential manner. When reflecting on the aforementioned stages, however, John expressed his sense of being overwhelmed with the various stages. To support John, his supervisor suggested that he begin slowly and work toward engaging his clients during the social stage of treatment. John was reminded that unless clients felt respected and understood, they are unlikely to return for counseling.

After a brief discussion with the supervisor, John began to view initial interviews as analogous to the arrival of visitors at his home. By doing so, John reflected on the natural process of welcoming friends into his home and ensuring that they felt comfortable through casual conversation and small talk. Using a similar approach with clients, John discovered that he was less anxious about having to move too quickly and getting down to clinical business. Consequently, he began to allow more time to welcome and engage clients. In short, he came to better appreciate the human element of counseling.

The Self-Assessment Instrument (Casey et al., 1989) consists of 13 tasks that cover a wide range of clinical tasks, as described in Table 1.2.

TABLE 1.2. Clinical Tasks

---

1. Establishing and maintaining an effective clinical and supervisory working relationship
2. Developing clinical goals and objectives
3. Developing and refining assessment skills
4. Developing and refining clinical management skills
5. Interacting in the clinical process
6. Observing and analyzing assessment and treatment
7. Developing and maintaining clinical records and supervisory records
8. Planning, executing, and analyzing supervisory conferences
9. Evaluating clinical performance
10. Demonstrating skills of verbal reporting, writing, and editing
11. Demonstrating knowledge of ethical; legal and regulatory; and reimbursement information
12. Demonstrating professional conduct
13. Demonstrating research skills in the clinical process.

Casey, Smith, and Ulrich, copyright 1989 in *Self-Supervision: A career tool for audiologists and speech–language pathologists*. Reprinted with permission of the National Student Speech Language Hearing Association.

Skills are assessed on a Likert scale ranging from 0 (not important/not applicable) to 10 (extremely important). To determine individual scores, a scoring system is provided. For example, 90% to100% signifies clinician satisfaction and command of a task area, 80% to 89% suggests that a clinician is getting by and needs to develop skills to a higher degree, 70% to 79% indicates that a clinician is struggling and that a task area demands increased attention, and finally, 69% or less implies that a clinician is struggling more than they should be and he or she needs to immediately work toward increasing his or her skills in that particular area. It does not appear that the validity or reliability of this instrument has been established. Nevertheless, this instrument does provide clinicians with a potentially useful tool.

☐ Cognitive Behavioral–Oriented Self-Supervision

Leith, McNiece, and Fusilier (1989) directly addressed self-supervision within a cognitive behavioral framework, stating:

> Self-supervision is the stuff that nurtures professional growth and effective and efficient treatment. As self-supervision becomes more proficient, there is less need for a supervisor to oversee the therapy and, hence, fewer clinical conferences. This in itself should provide the supervisee with motivation to hasten the development of self-supervision skills!" (p. 78)

In Leith et al.'s opinion, the most crucial skill supervisees can learn from supervisors is self-supervision, and without this skill, independent professional growth halts. When discussing a counselor's review of his or her responses in treatment and the overall transactions between counselors and clients, Leith et al. remarked:

> This is where the clinician does her problem solving, her self-supervision. It is here that she determines the effectiveness and efficiency of her treatment program. It is here that she makes adjustments and corrections in her therapy. She adjusts her therapy to meet the ever-changing needs, attitudes, emotions, and physical state of her client. She adjusts to shifts in the client's motivation, attitudes toward therapy, cooperation, and other factors that influence therapy. (p. 18)

According to Leith et al. (1989), for self-supervision to be effective, counselors must recognize clinical problems as they arise and possess the ability to solve these problems. Embedded in this process is the tremendous skill that underlies the process of *recognizing* subtle idiosyncrasies within the counseling relationship. Leith et al. remarked that counselors who self-supervise need to remain proactive, continually assess the counseling process, and remain vigilant to potential problems that can hinder treatment. They emphasized the need for counselors to develop observation and problem-solving skills and elaborated that a self-supervising counselor

> must consider all of the factors operating in the clinical interactions and, by carefully examining all the factors, determine if a relationship exists between them and the clinical problem she is facing. If she discovers a relationship, she will also discover how to deal with it." (p. 69)

Leith et al. (1989) contributed to the advancement in self-supervision theory and practice by alluding to the various teaching styles supervisors can employ when introducing self-supervision skills and through the creation of Clinical Session Self-Supervision, Diagnostic Session Self-Supervision, and Mid-Term/End-of-Term Self-Supervision forms. Each of the aforementioned styles can be employed with beginning, intermediate, advanced, and professional counselors. Each level has been differentiated by an actual number of clinical hours, for example, beginning level (0–100 hours), intermediate level (100–200 hours), advanced level (200–300 hours), and professional (beyond 300 hours). Leith et al. (1989) provided a "Key to Clinical Competency" for each level and outlined assigned scores regarding the quality of performance to each skill.

The Clinical Session Self-Supervision Form consists of 12 clinical competencies that are rated on a Likert scale that ranges from 1 (poor) to 5 (very good). Both interactions/management skills and procedures are considered. Interactions/management skills pertain to client engagement and counselor behavior. Procedural skills, on the other hand, specifically address clinical intervention (e.g., clinical goals, talk/response time, behavior change). The Diagnostic Session Self-Supervision Form focuses on planning, interactions, management, procedures, report writing, and other diagnostic responsibilities. The Mid-Term/End-of-Term Self-Supervision Form considers the areas of planning, clinical and supervisory interactions, management, procedures, and diagnosis. Program grade or rating for each form is determined by finding the average after calculating the amount of supervision and the quality of performance scores. In addition to quantitative data, qualitative information is gathered to provide a global picture of the counselor's work. Again, what remains unclear is the validity and reliability of these instruments.

☐ Counselor Self-Assessment

Bernard and Goodyear (1992, 1998) pointed to a trend in the literature toward self-assessment of clinical skills. They echoed Langs' (1979) earlier concern that little was being done to help counselors self-evaluate and Yager's (1987) contention about the lack of clinical supervision afforded counselors. In their opinion, self-assessment had become a critical skill for helping professionals. They further postulated that counselor self-assessment took away some of the parental authority from supervisors rather than adding to it.

To assist counselors in self-supervising their work, Yager and Park (1986) proposed a three-phase model comprising (a) self-assessment, (b) self-action, and (c) self-evaluation in a continuous feedback loop. In their opinion, this model could be useful in counselor skill development and in preventing burnout. The model is briefly described here and involves an assessment-action-evaluation process.

During the self-assessment phase, counselors consider their level of self-awareness and ask, What am I doing poorly, doing well, or doing not at all in my counseling responsibilities? Yager and Park (1986) wisely pointed out that this assessment might be extremely difficult for counselors who assume a multitude of responsibilities. The self-action phase involves steps to take to transform a counselor's newly discovered self-awareness into useful action. Yager and Park provided what they refer to as starter questions for counselors who are interested in gaining increased self-awareness and developing self-action plans, as described in Table 1.3.

In terms of the evaluation phase, counselors are encouraged to carefully review and assess each strategy they employ. Information that is obtained from the evaluation phase simply provides additional information that can go through the three-phase cycle again. Although Yager and Park (1986) did not comment on the effectiveness of their model, it is straightforward and provides counselors with a practical framework with which to assess their work.

☐ Self-Supervision in Systemic and Family Therapy

Several authors in the area of marriage and family therapy have contributed to the self-supervision literature. While some have merely alluded

---

TABLE 1.3. Potential Starter Questions

1. What is the focus of my functioning as a counselor?
2. Are there ways I can achieve the goals of my work by putting more time into preventative and developmental activities?
3. How self-reinforcing are the strategies I have been applying?
4. Given the desired activities identified, do I posses the skills necessary to implement them?
5. Is my plan realistic?

Taken from Yager, G., and Park, W. (1986).

to this process (e.g., Kaslow, 1986), others have tried to conceptualize a practice framework. Steiden (1993), for example, briefly described self-supervision using discourse analysis. Steiden found discourse analysis (talk about talk) to be helpful and wrote, "My first experience using discourse analysis as self-supervision helped me to see the ways I had made assumptions about clients' concerns based on initial interpretations of their talk" (p. 2). She further stated that the process of researching a text was instrumental in better understanding themes and concerns. Interestingly, Steiden suggested how this approach could help resolve a dissensus between counselors and clients:

> Rather than leave the dissensus dangling, the use of conversational and/or discourse analysis process might offer the clinicians opportunities to re-negotiate and/or close these unresolved moments. Either participant could offer the other a different interpretation of the situation from a new position of understanding. (p. 2)

Steiden pointed out that self-supervision is a deliberate activity that can assist counselors in rethinking their initial positions.

In drawing an analogy between qualitative interviewing and family therapy interviews, Chenail (1997) reviewed the strengths and weaknesses of self-supervision. Chenail pointed out that the self-supervision format can be a very effective and useful approach, but can also possess *dead characteristics*. On a positive note, he asserted that when using self-supervision, counselors, like researchers, are afforded opportunities to "take a break to clear their heads, review the interview as it has been unfolding, and make any mid-session corrections which may need to be made." Chenail went on to suggest that while self-supervising, counselors can "call upon their previous training and experience to help them make their current interview better." This former aspect is critical to the self-supervision process, in that counselors deliberately interrupt or slow down the counseling session to regain a sense of therapeutic direction. To do so, counselors rely on their training and experience.

In other words, rather than reacting to a situation, counselors prepare themselves to reflect and respond appropriately. Perhaps it is the ability to refrain from reacting, and to rather respond, which is at the crux of the self-supervision process. Realizing, either physiologically or emotionally, that an issue, remark, or event occurring in counseling has affected them, counselors can slow the process, reflect, and respond accordingly. The opposite would be a knee-jerk approach that is automatic and without reflection. It should be reiterated that reactions and responses can coincide with counseling issues, remarks, or events and can be perceived as negative and positive. For example, after being recognized by clients for their perceived insight and skill, counselors proudly accept and report this feedback without reflecting on why it was meaningful to them. Similarly, counselors who are informed that a client is terminating treatment prematurely may express disappointment and sense of failure without knowing why they feel this way. As noted earlier, both responses say something about the counselor.

When discussing dead characteristics, Chenail (1997) referred to counselor reflections that "only occur after an interview has been conducted, [and] the opportunity to be different in the interview itself has been lost." For its potential to be maximized, self-supervision should transpire during a counseling session or prearranged interludes.

O'Hanlon and Wilk (1987) remarked that counselors could evolve and grow through the self-supervision process. They suggested that when reviewing audio- and videotapes and recollections of a session, counselors could listen for "unchallenged presuppositions, imperatives, characterizations, and so on (both their clients' and their own)" (p. 262). They went on to note that counselors can

> note patterns of their own behavior, and can then vary these to find whether they have any effect on therapeutic outcome. If we are not getting results in a case, we may experiment by finding any regularity in our behavior and varying it to discover whether this alteration results in any beneficial effect." (p. 262)

It is important to underline that O'Hanlon and Wilk focused on the behavioral patterns of counselors and encouraged clinicians to become innovative and vary their behavior in search of better results.

O'Hanlon and Wilk (1987) reported that aside from occasional discussions with colleagues, self-supervision was the only form of supervision they themselves relied upon. These authors found themselves departing from traditional supervision for reasons often experienced by student counselors: They found that supervisors were inflexible and expected their supervisees to accept and believe in their presuppositions and imperatives. To no one's surprise, the success of the supervision process largely rested on the nature and quality of supervision.

Keller and Protinsky (1984) proposed a self-management model for family therapy supervision, integrating several approaches into a model of supervision that emphasizes "increasing self-awareness and the therapeutic management-of-self in the clinical setting" (p. 281). Based on family-of-origin, family constellation, and Adlerian frameworks, counselors were invited to revisit family patterns that were learned in the past and interrupt problematic patterns of interaction that inhibit their clinical work. This work is closely related to the work of McDaniel and Landau-Stanton (1991) that will be reviewed later.

Keller and Protinsky's (1984) model of self-management involved a series of steps including (a) presentation of a three-generation family of origin and a review of patterns (e.g., triangulation and fusion), (b) collection and presentation of family constellation material (e.g., sibling order, gender, age differences between siblings), (c) a group review with supervisor and peers regarding primary management-of-self patterns in interactional contexts, (d) presentation and scrutiny of a videotaped therapy case for management-of-self strategies, and finally (e) the direct application of various options for increasing the effectiveness of management-of-self strategies (e.g., monitoring intrapersonal, interpersonal, and contextual cues). According to Keller and Protinsky, their supervision model emphasized "the understanding and integration of trainees beliefs in their families-of-origin. This integration can then provide very useful guidelines for the use-of-self supervisory process" (p. 287).

Based on constructive inquiry and embedded narratives, Lowe (2000) offered a model of supervision of self-supervision. In describing his approach, Lowe preferred to use the alternative term *self-sustaining*, as opposed to self-supervising. From his perspective:

> Self-sustaining therapists assume a proactive responsibility for their own supervisory needs and ongoing professional development. They feel confident to practice in the absence of routine formal supervision but also feel competent to discern when their own reflections need to be enhanced through consultation with a supervisor, colleagues, peers, or other professionals." (p. 512)

In essence, Lowe's (2000) approach involves the active participation of supervisors in assisting counselors to develop their self-supervision skills. Supervisors use what are referred to as *expert wonderings* that are designed to facilitate conversations with counselors and highlight their expertise. Lowe identified and elaborated on the stages of his supervision of self-supervision model. The stages of this model include goal setting and prioritizing, appreciating competence and change, identifying challenges and resources, contributing from the supervisor's frame, preparing for future casework, and finally, reflecting on the case consultation.

Within family therapy, Todd (1997b, 1992) has made the greatest attempt to articulate and develop a self-supervision model. He discussed self-supervision as a universal goal when training marriage and family therapists. Toward this end, he wrote, "As gatekeepers of marriage and family therapy and other mental health professions, supervisors are expected to prepare supervisees for self-supervision or for practicing without supervision. Clearly most supervisors would prefer to think of their task as the former" (Todd, 1997b, p. 19). Although suspecting that most marriage and family therapy supervisors would consider self-sufficiency an ultimate goal for supervisees, Todd (1997b) remarked on the lack of attention and guidelines pertaining to the practice of self-supervision. He suggested that the lack of attention rendered to self-supervision may be due to the fact that most graduate and postgraduate MFT programs generally do not expect their students to be self-sufficient upon graduation. In other words, despite advanced theory courses, training, and clinical supervision, students are still required to seek close monitoring of their work. In addressing the expectations of MFT students, Mead (1990) noted that supervisors could help students learn to analyze the entire counseling context by evaluating personal history, the clinical setting, clients, administrative constraints, and counselor-supervisor interaction. According to Mead (1990), counselors could become truly self-supervising, which in his opinion was "one mark of the expert therapist" (p. 112). Lowe (2000) echoed this view and stated that, "Indeed, the gradual transition to self-supervision, with therapists taking increasing responsibility for identifying and voicing their supervision needs, can be seen as a hallmark of professional development" (p. 512).

Todd (1997b) defined self-supervision as, "a process whereby therapists self-monitor their therapeutic behavior, comparing this behavior with some model of more effective behavior, with the intent of changing their behavior to resemble this model more closely" (p. 18). When we contrast this definition with the early work of Langs (1979), it initially appears that Todd's focus was on having supervisees change unwanted behavior while working toward assuming behaviors that would prove to be more effective. Langs, on the other hand, embraced a larger perspective and encouraged supervisees to also identify and punctuate strengths. After learning more about Todd's model, however, it becomes evident that he too encouraged supervisees to "conduct their own *search* [italics in original] of assets and skills to find the resources to succeed in therapy" (p. 20). It is interesting to note that what Langs had promoted as a framework for supervision years ago was eventually referred to as solution-focused supervision (Juhnke, 1996; Marek, Sandifer, Beach, Coward, & Protinsky, 1994; Storm, 1995b; Thomas, 1994; Todd, 1997a; Wetchler, 1990).

In addition to explicating a model of self-supervision, Todd (1997b) refers to the concept of self-reflexivity. In doing so, he reemphasized the interpretative, reciprocal, systemic processes within the therapeutic context. Rather than perceiving clients as solely responsible for the outcome of treatment, counselors are invited to consider a systemic framework and think about how their assumptions, thoughts, emotions, and behaviors influence their interactions with clients. As proposed within the principles of second-order cybernetics (Keeney, 1983), the perceptions, cognitions, and behaviors of all participants in the counseling relationship contribute to mutual triggering events that can lead to conflictual interactions. In other words, it would be erroneous for counselors to see themselves as apart from the therapeutic context. In fact, they are inexorably intertwined with clients.

Along with other counselor educators, Todd (1997b) suggested the use of technology to gain information about one's clinical skills. For example, clinicians could review videotapes of their work. He cited several frameworks that could be employed in conjunction with a video review to assess intervention and included Kagan's (1980) model of IPR, Steiden's (1993) use of discourse analysis, Schwartz's (1995) model of Internal Family Systems, and the use of genograms (Baverman, 1984; Kuehl, 1996).

The use of video review to enhance the self-supervision process was also endorsed by Haber (1996). When helping family therapy students develop their self-supervision skills, he would first invite them to pretend that they were behind a one-way mirror observing the case they were presenting and then ask questions such as, "What generates your concern about the interview?"; "Why do you think the therapist intervenes in this manner?"; "What suggestions would you make?"; "How do you think the therapist and the family would respond to the suggested interventions?" Haber suggests that therapists can pretend that they are supervising themselves from behind a one-way mirror. Therapists who have had the opportunity of being supervised within this context may still recall the advice of mentors who effectively slowed down the therapeutic process, diffused anxious moments, and encouraged a pensive posture. The ultimate goal was to create avenues for change and restore a sense of latitude and optimism.

Two things are apparent in Haber's (1996) efforts when promoting student self-supervision. First, there is the invitation for students to assume a metaposition to their own work. Along similar lines advocated by Langs (1979), students are encouraged to step out of their clinical role, temporarily suspend their thinking, and consider new perspectives. Second, Haber emphasized the need for students to develop a *critical eye* within a safe and empowering learning environment. When inviting students to take risks, Haber realized the need for students to feel respected. Unfortunately, aside from outlining several questions that he posed to students, Haber did not elaborate on the self-supervision process in more detail.

In what appears to be a strong endorsement for self-supervision, Patterson, Williams, Grauf-Grounds, and Chamow (1998) suggested that family therapists "should develop self-reflective methods and questions that could be used in place of getting supervision from another individual" (p. 200). Patterson et al. proposed reviewing videotapes of their work and developing self-supervision questions. Potential questions are included in Table 1.4.

A fundamental concept within Todd's (1997b) model of self-supervision is a search for the *Ideal Model*. In other words, supervisees are encouraged

---

TABLE 1.4. Potential Self-Supervision Questions

---

1. Am I, as the therapist, working harder than the clients?
2. What are negative consequences of change with which my clients may be struggling?
3. Does the problem serve some positive function or purpose?
4. Have I clearly assessed the client's goals, and does the client see me as working toward those goals?
5. Have I sufficiently joined with the client?
6. Does the client see therapy or the therapist as credible?
7. Is my frustration a possible sign of my own personal issues interfering with the client's?
8. Are my reactions or responses isomorphic to the system?
9. Have I appropriately balanced the responsibility for change? (Or do I find myself siding with one person over the other?)
10. Have I identified two or three key therapeutic issues or themes, or am I trying to focus on too many things?

Taken from Patterson, P., Williams, L., Grauf-Grounds, C., and Chamow, L. (1998). Reprinted with permission of Brunner-Routledge.

---

to "compare their actual therapeutic behavior with some idealized norm. Therapists could compare videotapes of their work with images from training videotapes of master therapists. The *model* [italics in original] also could come from the therapist's own behavior rather than that of a master therapists" (p. 18).

The self-supervision guidelines set forth by Todd (1997b) provide supervisors and supervisees with a foundation upon which to establish a working relationship and vision. Guidelines include establishing (a) self-supervision as an overall goal, (b) a collaborative partnership, (c) a list of perceptual, conceptual, and executive skills, and (d) methods by which to achieve skills. Within his proposed guidelines, Todd discussed the different learning styles among supervisees. In order for supervisors and supervisees to establish a collaborative relationship, it is imperative that preferred learning styles of supervisees be identified. He also pointed out that not all supervisees understand their personal learning style. In these cases, it is a supervisor's responsibility to assist supervisees in beginning to understand how they best learn. To make self-supervision a useful experience, Todd promoted an atmosphere filled with questions and curiosity. Further, he advocated small, incremental steps to supervisee development.

Todd (1997b) did not address issues that arise when there is a poor match between supervisor and supervisee. Obviously, not all supervisees are in the enviable position of selecting a supervisor who is willing to accommodate his or her learning style. More is said about this in Chapter 5.

Comparable to asking supervisees to articulate their learning style, Todd (1997b) underscored the rigor involved in self-supervision and suggested that supervisees (a) begin to identify the theoretical framework that guides their clinical work, (b) scan their work for therapeutic errors, (c) identify videotaped case material that illustrates their assets and resources, and (d) continually explain how their clinical work relates to established treatment goals. In keeping with the age of therapeutic accountability, Todd also encouraged seeking honest client feedback on therapy. This approach can be coupled with follow-up surveys to determine the effectiveness of therapy.

☐ Self-Supervision within a Group Context

Although self-supervision is generally perceived as an independent enterprise, or one between supervisor and supervisees, attempts to use this process within a different context have been addressed. A. Williams (1995), for example, wrote of his model of group supervision:

> The goal of group supervision is the development of collective and individual clinical wisdom: technical and procedural knowledge, judgement, and perspicacity. The group works together to develop the role of *self-consultant* [italics in original] in each member, so that each of them becomes a self-monitoring professional and remains so after the supervision period ends. (p. 212)

Within the group supervision context referred to by Williams, doubts, uncertainties, and questions are expressed and encouraged. Unfortunately, Williams stopped short and only provided marginal details regarding self-monitoring in his supervision groups.

☐ Self-Supervision in Psychiatry

Lewis (1991) elaborated on his efforts to introduce psychiatric residents to the process of self-monitoring early in their medical training. By doing so, he hoped that the self-monitoring process would eventually become routine practice and emphasized the importance of a systematic format within which counselors could examine their own work.

The self-monitoring process outlined by Lewis (1979) centered on the dual positions (objective and empathic) of counselors when working with clients. The *objective* position referred to the emotional distance or detachment counselors maintain when focusing on client psychopathology. It was assumed that, by remaining the emotionally distant, counselors would be in an efficacious position to understand and influence client behavior. With this stance, the focus is placed on the observational processes involved in counseling (e.g., client associations, recognition of nonverbal signals, identification of defense mechanisms). Lewis (1991) theorized that assuming a detached position permitted a counselor to "bring together his or her observations and inferences in the form of a clinical formulation" (p. 143). Armed with this formulation, clinicians could then be expected to intervene appropriately.

The *empathic* position emphasizes a counselor's sensitivity to affective messages and the empathic process. Lewis (1991) contended that clients' empathic messages could arouse similar affective states within counselors. When discussing this process, Lewis commented that, "The affective arousal of the therapists may take the form of an affectively laden fantasy or memory or even a relatively content-free affective state" (p. 143). According to Lewis, the empathic process can occur spontaneously, or it can be influenced deliberately by counselors who wish to abandon a detached position and begin to enter a client's experience. The close emotional proximity between clients and counselors that can develop within this latter relationship may require special attention to ensure that client-professional boundaries are respected and maintained (Edelwich & Brodsky, 1991; Heyward, 1993; Peterson, 1992; Strean, 1993).

As pointed out by Lewis (1991), some counselors begin to divert from a customary detachment position in order to enter the client's experience without having any sense of where they are going. This latter point is critical. Diverting from a treatment plan without knowing why they are moving into a different clinical direction can place counselors and clients in a vulnerable position. Without careful reflection and consideration of triggering events or the recall of personal affective experiences, counselors may find themselves gravitating to issues that may hold personal worth yet are less important to client growth. Therefore, it is vital for counselors to know why they choose to pursue a specific issue or topic during the therapeutic hour. This point is not made to suggest that counselors should remain rigid and apprehensive toward changing the direction of treatment in what may be the best interests of clients. Rather, I am suggesting that professionals should be able to explain why they decided to abandon an original plan and change direction.

In my experience, counselors who independently sway from the original treatment plan are generally unaware of doing so. When reviewing a videotape of the session, they are surprised to see how they moved away from their agenda. Such behavior can result from memories of a painful history, personal trauma, or unresolved issues. What becomes evident in these situations are issues relating to the person-of-the-counselor, which will be discussed in Chapter 3. A convergence of personal stories begins to influence the content and direction of treatment.

To remain vigilant, Lewis (1991) suggested that counselors systematically and periodically monitor (a) their clinical formulation, (b) their affective arousal and (c) the distribution of power within the counseling relationship. To help counselors self-monitor their work, Lewis recommended asking two primary questions. The first question, "How can I understand the patient's predicament?", is first asked following the initial interview but should remain a constant throughout the counseling process. Although seemingly straightforward, this question sets into motion a counselor's clinical formulation and how he or she perceives the problem. Lewis suggested that counselors write an outline of the formulation for tracking purposes. The second question is, "How has my initial formulation been modified by the emerging data of psychotherapy?" Said in another way, counselors examine whether they are able to reformulate a client's dilemma based on the additional clinical information they have obtained. In essence, this exercise informs counselors about their ability to remain tentative and open to new information and, as Lewis (1979) stated, to "the increasing complexity of the task of reformulation" (p. 22). An inability to reformulate client dilemmas may indicate that counselors are unable to recognize and integrate new clinical information and are unaware of their reactions to clients. Generally, counselors who find themselves in this position have ignored or underestimated the interactional process of counseling and have miscalculated their influence.

Finally, Lewis (1991) recommended that counselor self-monitoring can focus on the distribution of power within the therapeutic relationship. A shift from a collaborative relationship to a relationship where counselors exude power is of particular concern. As noted earlier, counselors who become controlling may be reacting to a sense of incompetency.

In response to the rapidly changing health care system and decreased time for supervision, Winer and Klamen (1997) introduced another variation of self-supervision among psychiatric residents. These authors were interested in developing increased supervisory efficiency and effectiveness. Consequently, they developed a model wherein psychiatric residents trained within a traditional supervision framework while supervising themselves by audiotaping their sessions with clients, listening to each tape in its entirety independently, and making process notes based on what they heard. Residents were instructed to "paraphrase and summarize the patient's words and to write down *verbatim* [italics in original] what the therapist says" (p. 142). Following completion of this task, residents brought their notes to a regular supervision session and read their notes line by line. The *process notes* referred to by Winer and Klamen should not be confused with counselor *progress notes*. The latter are completed at various times following an interview and are generally sketchy and based on recall. Consequently, progress notes can be subject to distortion and omissions. Winer and Klamen argued that "supervision should be based on harder data provided by audiorecording" (p. 143).

According to Winer and Klamen (1997), there are several practical and professional benefits and limitations associated with this form of supervision. On a positive and practical level, residents who followed this format arrive prepared for supervision. Experienced supervisors understand how important this can be. Individuals who have prepared to delve into their work save valuable time and contribute to an ambiance of rigor and professionalism. Such individuals tend to be less reliant on supervisors for direction. Also, they have a better idea of their clinical and supervisory needs.

Counselors who prepare notes are also more likely to remain focused on a specific case that they are presenting. In the characteristically chaotic work of counseling, it is not difficult for clinicians to lose focus, get sidetracked, and begin to discuss extraneous information.

On a professional level, residents reported independent learning and an enhanced self-awareness while listening to their tapes. Residents commented on how they became increasingly cognizant of their techniques, strengths and weaknesses. It is important to note that the residents were particularly impressed with the fact that their newfound awareness was spontaneous and self-generated. Two advantages of this discovery include personal empowerment and the possible acceleration of supervision. That is, given the appropriate context, clinicians begin to realize they have an innate ability to independently discover aspects of themselves. Also, counselors who uncover important aspects of themselves prior to formal supervision are in a position to supplement their learning.

Winer and Klamen (1997) also discussed how their proposed self-supervision model decreases a resident's sense of vulnerability and helps to

> protect the often fragile self-esteem of the fledgling psychotherapist by having him or her preview the tape before the supervisory session, allowing the resident to *warn* [italics in original] the supervisor that a particularly difficult part in the therapy is coming up next in a resident's notes. (p.143)

In short, these authors reported that residents experience increased control and are more protected from external criticism when presenting their work.

To provide a balanced perspective, Winer and Klamen (1997) pointed out the limitations of their proposed self-supervision model. They included the resistance of some counselors to writing process notes and the amount of time necessary to transcribe information from audiotapes. While acknowledging these limitations, they suggested that, "Once the resident observes that coming to supervision with notes from an audiotaped session allows the resident to endure less injury to self-esteem and to experience more a sense of effectiveness, this method becomes self-reinforcing" (p. 143).

In terms of being time consuming, Winer and Klamen (1997) noted that it was not necessary for counselors to transcribe each and every session. In fact, counselors may decide to transcribe sections of a session or different types of sessions. For example, counselors who find it difficult to close a session may find it beneficial to record and transcribe the latter part of their sessions in order to detect patterns. Counselors who struggle with serving a specific client population may decide to record and transcribe tapes related to such clients.

An interesting distinction emerges within the aforementioned proposed model. It has to do with supervisory attention that is directed toward clinical case goals or personal development goals. Although there is an obvious overlap, there is also a major difference. In reference to self-supervision, counselor and supervisor attention needs to be directed toward personal development that leads to professional growth. Consequently, the primary purpose of reviewing clinical material is to enhance counselor self-awareness, not to devise a new strategy. To do the latter would be to miss the mark in the context of self-supervision. This is precisely why there is a degree of vulnerability involved in this process: The focus is on the counselor, not the client(s).

The idea of having counselors select tape segments, albeit videotape segments, for review and discussion is not new and was discussed by Breulin, Karper, McGuire, and Cimmarusti (1988). These authors emphasized the need for focus to increase learning potential and asserted that goals should be precise, limited in scope, and operationalized. And, as noted by Winer and Klamen (1997), specifying goals provides a clear task and clear expectations and can reduce counselor anxiety because they know their work will not be scrutinized.

☐ Conclusion

A historical review of the literature pertaining to self-supervision demonstrates that over the years various clinicians from a number of helping professions have recognized its value and potential to varying degrees. An interesting finding in addition to several terms used to describe self-supervision was that the individuals who pursued the development of this innovative process did so independently of one another. With a few exceptions, although each individual represented a helping profession, they did not appear to collaborate in articulating or formalizing this practice.

Several methods and assessment instruments have been designed to assist counselors when self-supervising. The development of assessment instruments is critical to the practical operationalization, future research, and increased creditability of self-supervision. Moving self-supervision from an abstract notion to an activity that can actually be practiced has enormous benefits for helping professionals and their clients.

☐ Review/Discussion Questions

1. List the names of prominent figures who contributed to the development of self-supervision.
2. What is the underlying purpose of self-supervision?
3. Identify and contrast instruments that are designed to evaluate the self-supervision process.
4. What benefits are associated with self-supervision?

2

The Counselor-Client Relationship

Therapy is a deeply intimate and vulnerable experience, requiring sensitivity to one's own state of being as well as to that of the other. It is the meeting of the deepest self of the therapists with the deepest self of the patient or client.

—Virginia Satir, 1987

A positive counselor-client relationship is critical to any treatment plan. Without this fundamental component, treatment is unlikely to succeed. As counselors reflect on their relationships with clients during the self-supervision process, it is important that they consider their level of involvement and personal behaviors. More specifically, the development of counselor overinvolvement and how remaining fixed in this position can potentially impede therapeutic goals and cause counselor-client conflict deserves attention (Butler & Bird, 2000; Friesen & Casella, 1982; Kerr & Bowen, 1988; Kuypers & Trute, 1980; Lynch, 1981; Titleman, 1992; Zupan, Babcock, & Morrissette, 1988).

☐ Counselor Centrality and Overinvolvement

The first step in better understanding counselor centrality and overinvolvement involves conceptualizing the counseling relationship wherein both sides contribute to the treatment process. Simply depicting clients as culprits who intentionally draw counselors into their problems is disrespectful of clients and too shallow of an explanation.

Subscribing to a linear perspective wherein one side is held responsible for the lack of clinical progress or a strained counselor-client relationship also ignores the bidirectional process of counseling. To provide counselors with an alternative way to deconstruct the counseling relationship and to better understand their participation and contributions, a systemic per-spective is offered.

☐ Overinvolvement Through a Systemic Lens

The concept of overinvolvement can be understood as a series of interactional invitations that take place between counselors and clients. For example, a client's seemingly helpless disposition can be a wonderful invitation for counselors to prove their caring and worth by becoming more involved. This increased involvement in turn becomes an invitation for clients to remain or grow even more helpless and dependent upon clinicians. Often, counselors who possess fragile egos and who succumb to pressures to perform or succeed can find themselves deeply invested in creating or maintaining client harmony. They exaggerate their importance, gradually become overly invested in client problems, and perceive themselves as key players and central figures who prevent client regression. It is not unusual, for example, to hear counselors proudly announce that they have provided clients with their home telephone numbers, have met with clients after hours (even in precarious situations) to defuse a potentially critical incident, or have simply gone beyond the call of duty. Such counselors begin to depict themselves as altruists who serve as intermediaries between a client's mental health and emotional demise. Both novice and seasoned counselors can assume a self-inflated view of themselves and can contribute to inappropriate counselor participation, inhibit client growth, and protract treatment. Both novice and experienced counselors disclose their dissatisfaction with current models of counseling and counselor behaviors that seem emotionally cold. In their opinion, clients need to know that they are valued and cared about, and it is the responsibility of clinicians to ensure that clients feel accepted and protected. Their narratives are filled with passion for and devotion to clients. Unfortunately, clients can also perceive these narratives as condescending or patronizing. In other words, a counselor's self-appointed position of power can be reflective of their need to be in a superior position in relation to clients. Under these circumstances, counselors are less devoted to the growth and development of their clients than they are to their own need to be recognized and acknowledged. Maslach (1982) suggested that, "Getting overly involved with people also occurs when those people satisfy some personal needs—such as a need for attention or rec-ognition or appreciation of some sort" (p. 33).

Further, counselors who claim altruistic motives may be overlooking the costs associated with their behavior. Although counselor self-care is addressed in more detail in Chapter 6, the implications associated with overextending oneself cannot be overemphasized. As counselors devote substantial amounts of time and energy to helping clients, they may lose sight of their own personal health and the needs of their own families. Only after suffering ill health, or when experiencing family problems, do they realize that their priorities were mismanaged. This process generally takes place over a period of time and is characterized by counselors spend-ing extra time at work and less time caring for themselves and their families.

Case Vignette

Having moved up to a supervisory position in a child/adolescent group home, Bonnie was adamant about doing her job well and setting an example for the child care staff. When she was a child care worker she often complained about the daily opera-tion of the group home and vowed that she would make the necessary changes if she became supervisor. As supervisor, she now had the opportunity to put her well-thought-out plans into action. During the first few weeks, the child care staff sup-ported and reacted positively to Bonnie's new ideas. To her delight, team morale was improving and initial feedback from the staff was very encouraging. To main-tain this trend, Bonnie frequently stayed a few minutes after work to help out her colleagues and spend time with the children. The staff appreciated her energy, assis-tance, and commitment.

Feeling valued and integral to the program's stability, Bonnie began to forgo her after-work exercise routine in order to devote more time to the group home. She justified her behavior to herself and her husband by telling him that her colleagues and the children at the group home needed her. Gradually, and despite spending an enormous amount of time at work, Bonnie was noticing that the old patterns that she once criticized were returning. Feeling unappreciated Bonnie began to argue with her colleagues and would often return home feeling angry and overwhelmed. Despite pleas from her husband to reduce her involvement with the child care staff and return to a normal workday, Bonnie was convinced that she had to try harder. Within a short period of time, complaints about Bonnie's administrative style grew and she was asked to meet with the Program Director.

Unbeknownst to counselors, their overinvolvement can occur very gradually and become problematic. Further, an attempted solution can become the problem. Rather than stepping back and reassessing strained relationships with clients or colleagues, they remain determined and per-sist in applying strategies that have proven unsuccessful. As counselors become immersed in their work, they often sacrifice their personal well-being and intimate or social relationships to alleviate their anxiety or in search of professional recognition. Instead of delegating responsibility and protecting important boundaries, counselors accept innocuous invitations to become overinvolved and, eventually, consumed by their work. More seasoned counselors who experience life-changing events (e.g., suicide of a family member) can sometimes find themselves atypically hypervigilant and overinvolved in cases in which client welfare and safety is questionable. Despite their clinical experience and knowledge of therapeutic boundaries, personal life events influence and can distort a professional's perspective. In response to their own needs, they become unknowingly overinvolved with clients. Because clients become vulnerable when boundaries are transgressed, it is important to understand that their participation should be carefully monitored and occur only at strategic points in treatment. By doing so, clients are afforded ample time and space to grow without counselor interference.

☐ Oversteping Boundaries

Overinvolved counselors are usually unaware or lose sight of therapeutic boundaries. As a result, they find themselves situated at a disadvantageous position and become temporarily handicapped. In essence, such counselors have intruded on therapeutic boundaries that exist between them and clients. This transgression is usually displayed by counselors who attempt to do things for clients that the clients could do independently or with minimal assistance. Although counselors should assume responsibility for organizing treatment, they must also remain cognizant of how easy it is to hinder treatment by becoming unnecessarily involved in client decisions. Counselors should avoid assuming responsibility for a client's decisions and actions, thereby preventing therapeutic entanglement. In conceptualizing the therapeutic process systemically, Keeney (1979) stated:

> Perhaps the most important idea in cybernetics and systems theory today is that mutual, reciprocal, simultaneous interactions define, identify, and constitute whole systems. This view follows the axiom of ecology and systems theory that all parts within a system simultaneously act on one another. For example, as the therapist acts on the identified patient, the identified patient acts on the therapists in a simultaneous fashion. It is the simultaneous interactions between therapist and identified patient (and all other parts of the therapeutic situation) that characterize a whole system. (p. 123)

Clinicians who subscribe to a systemic perspective attempt to maintain that perspective and adequate maneuverability throughout treatment. From the outset, it is important that counselors beware of creating a context wherein patterns of overinvolvement and inadvertent dependency may develop. This process begins with the initial telephone call (DiBlasio, Fischer, & Prata, 1986). How counselors begin the therapeutic relationship and set the tone for future interactions will impact their work.

Initial telephone calls are much more valuable than simply gaining demographic information and setting appointment times. When speaking with clients for the first time, the establishment of boundaries can begin and pertinent information can be obtained that can be instrumental in engaging clients and designing the intervention. It is necessary for counselors to ask important questions, search for clues that can augment treatment, and begin establishing counselor-client boundaries. In terms of boundaries, it is not uncommon for prospective clients to request that counselors call them to remind them about their scheduled appointment times or provide transportation to and from the session. Counselors who agree to these requests might benefit from asking themselves a few simple questions: Why am I doing things for clients that they could do for themselves? Whose needs are being met? Why am I becoming overly invested in ensuring client welfare?

Some counselors also use the initial telephone call to start the therapeutic process. For instance, counselors might ask clients to begin a very basic personal genogram and timeline prior to the first interview as an information-gathering exercise. The purpose of the exercise is at least threefold. First, clients are immediately immersed and active in the clinical process. They quickly learn that they will be expected to actively participate and complete assignments during treatment. Rather than perceiving themselves as passive participants, they are invited to assume a collaborative role. Second, they are given an opportunity to delve into their own history. Some clients who have completed a rudimentary genogram arrive for their first interview enthusiastically reporting newly discovered knowledge (e.g., patterns) about their families and themselves. Third, if they follow the request to complete a genogram, they are already immersed in the treatment process, which can save valuable clinical time.

☐ Transitional Points in Counseling

Initially, counselors work toward understanding client patterns and ride the counseling merry-go-round. During the course of treatment, however, counselors must know at which strategic transitional points to jump off the merry-go-round and allow clients to operate independently to self-correct. Overinvolvement should not be perceived as a stagnant position, but rather as a position that can be moved away from as easily as it was moved into. This ebb-and-flow process reflects the ever-changing needs, attitudes, emotions, and physical states of clients. What can be added, of course, are similar changes among counselors. Combined, counseling can be seen as an endeavor that is in constant motion.

This perspective is quite different from the lineal-causal view of counselors who are inducted into the client system or trapped by clients. The counseling system is constantly in flux, so overinvolvement need be only a temporary position, which, when recognized during self-supervision, can be corrected. It should be remembered that just as counselors can get stuck therapeutically with clients, clients can get stuck therapeutically with counselors.

Case Vignette

After six sessions with Lou, a community counselor, Joy explained that she was feeling much better about her oldest son moving away from home despite his poor employment prospects. She explained that the family-of-origin work she participated in was very useful and helped to clarify her position in relation to her son. Expecting to terminate counseling after the agreed-upon six sessions, Joy was surprised when Lou suggested that they revisit their original counseling contract. Lou elaborated that Joy's reaction to her son might be symbolic of deep-rooted intrapersonal issues that, if not resolved, could manifest in other relationships. Lou further stated that he was worried that Joy's progress could be jeopardized or even erased if she terminated treatment prematurely. As she listened to Lou, Joy's confidence slowly dwindled. Although she was less concerned about her future, Lou remained adamant and persuasive.

The preceding case vignette illustrates both counselor influence and how clinicians can become more concerned about client problems than clients themselves. Many factors can effect a counselor's position in relation to the presenting problem including the meaning associated with the problem (e.g., did Lou have a traumatic experience with another client in a similar situation? Did he experience difficulty during the leaving-home stage with his own child?), the context (e.g., did Lou feel pressured to solve the case? Did he need to maintain a specific caseload to secure his employment?), and the relationship to clients (e.g., was Lou feeling protective of Joy? Was he sexually attracted to her?)

Counselors may experience a range of unusual emotions and behaviors when working with specific clients. As noted below, these emotions and behaviors may indicate counselor overinvolvement.

☐ Indicators of Counselor Overinvolvement

Clinical indicators suggesting overinvolvement may be very subtle and, as a result, not always obvious to counselors. Case presentations can often reveal counselors' protectiveness and hypervigilance vis-a-vis clients. Emotionally charged adjectives used by counselors in describing clients usually indicate an overinvolved position. Also, as discussed later, counselor tone and language indicating overinvolvement can progress and contribute to hostile and nontherapeutic environments.

A reluctance to present a client for case review or supervision can indicate a *closed door* attitude by counselors. In some instances, counselors are so protective of clients that they avoid discussing client information or clinical status. In such situations, it appears that counselors feel that clients need to be guarded and shielded against other professionals. Clinicians who assume this position are like sentinels protecting their territory, and they consider even the most benign recommendation threatening. Counselors who are initially reluctant to review particular cases may find that self-supervision provides them with a private context within which to reflect and consider options.

Case Vignette

As a part of their professional development plan, the clinicians at a psychotherapy institute decided to set aside one morning each week to present cases that required additional input. It was agreed in principle that a rotational system would be instituted, thus allowing everyone an opportunity to present a case either verbally, through audiotape review, or through a live presentation with the use of a one-way mirror.

When Alan's presentation time arrived, he apologized for not having a case to present. In his opinion, he was doing quite well with the exception of a couple of clients in the outreach project for disadvantaged clients. Alan thanked his colleagues for their support but did not feel that it was necessary to discuss the cases with which he was struggling. Alan's colleagues applauded his fine work and reputation within the institute and suggested that different perspectives could sometimes tweak new thinking. Growing defensive, Alan reminded his colleagues that he grew up disadvantaged and understood the unique needs of clients from this culture. He further asserted that "his people" [emphasis added] were often misunderstood and needed to be buffered from helpers who could not possibly understand their plight.

The above case example demonstrates how counselors can become very protective and overinvolved in their work. By discounting potentially useful information from colleagues, well-intentioned counselors may not be considering the best interests of their clients. Feeling that they alone can help a specific client or client population places professionals and clients in a precarious situation. As will be discussed below, remaining unaware of blind spots can hinder a counselor's therapeutic efforts and jeopardize treatment.

Several hypotheses can be generated regarding why counselors become overinvolved with clients. For example, counselors may become overinvolved in cases that stir up memories and become personally meaningful. Counselors might also display extraordinary concern with specific populations. One hypothesis that merits consideration, however, pertains to counselor self-esteem and self-protection. Counselors who feel that they have something to prove and a reputation to uphold tend to place unnecessary pressure on themselves and their clients. Rather than allowing the counseling process to naturally unfold, these counselors react to their self-imposed anxiety and intervene without careful reflection.

During counseling sessions, evidence of overinvolvement can be demonstrated verbally, nonverbally, physically, or physiologically by counselors. Of course, professionals may experience signs of overinvolvement to varying degrees. Examples of some different forms of counselor overinvolvement are given in the following case examples.

Verbal Indicators

Protective Tactics (Rescuing Client)

Case Vignette

During a family-school case conference, a school counselor began making excuses for why the parents were not following through on agreed-upon after-school consequences for their adolescent daughter. When the parents were confronted by the principal, who was threatening suspension, the school counselor would interject and offer various reasons why the parents were unable to fulfill their parental obligations and commitment to the school. Unknowingly, the school counselor was transgressing boundaries, assuming responsibility for the actions of the parents, and blocking opportunities for the parents to become accountable.

Inappropriate Participation

Case Vignette

During a couples therapy session that was being supervised through a one-way mirror, a counselor was directed by her supervisor to have the couple speak directly to one another about a contentious issue. The counselor followed the directive but became uneasy when the couple entered into a fervid debate. To ease her own anxiety, the counselor began to intrude on the conversation with light humor in an effort to lower the perceived tension in the room. Under the guise of a mediator, the counselor was responding to her own discomfort and inappropriately interfering with the couple's interaction.

Nonverbal Indicators

Feeling Restricted in Physical Movement

Case Vignette

During a family therapy interview, family members were discussing whether a young-ster who had attempted suicide should be released from the hospital and returned home. In response to the heavy mood within the room and the impending decision, the counselor remained motionless, with bated breath, frozen in his seat. Rather than remaining in a position from which he could freely move in and out of the family system, the counselor was drawn into the drama and was effectively para-lyzed by the gravity of the impending decision.

Facial or Body Expressions

The counselor may reflect the client's mood or feel personally worried, anxious, disappointed, etc.

Case Vignette

A pediatric social worker who was working with a youngster diagnosed with cancer was asked to speak to a single mother about her irregular visits and perceived lack of interest in support groups. As a way of breaking the ice, the social worker listed the boy's many fine qualities and shared how some parents would experience an increased closeness to their children during times of illness. While speaking with the mother, the social worker experienced increased anxiety and became unusually tense. Noticing that the mother was not immediately responding as she had hoped she would, the social worker was unsure of what to do and became very nervous.

Physical Indicators

Physical Contact

The counselor may engage in excessive touching, caressing, or hand-holding.

Case Vignette

A female counselor at a women's shelter was interacting with a woman who was considering returning to a violent relationship. As the client struggled in the delib-eration process, she covered her face and began to cry. In response, the counselor immediately moved her chair closer to the client and began to gently rub her back. That is, without permission from the client, the counselor moved into the client's physical and emotional space and touched her. The counselor was behaving in a way that she considered natural and harmless.

Physiological Indicators

Tenseness

This can present itself as headaches, nervousness, or nausea experienced by the counselor either before, during, or after counseling sessions.

Case Vignette

A couple who had decided to separate sought counseling to assist them in revealing their recent decision to their children. Before the interview, as she thought about the potential ramifications associated with the couple's decision, the counselor became very nervous and nauseated. Based on a previous experience, the counselor began to generalize about the future turmoil that children from divorced families experience.

Mood Deviation

The counselor may become sad, listless, angry, etc.

Case Vignette

A counselor who was employed by a foster care program was conducting an interview with a foster family who had experienced several behavioral outbursts and wanted to relinquish care of the child. As he listened to the foster parents, he periodically glanced over to the child, who was slipping deeper into his chair with each account. In response to the stories and the child's forlorn appearance and depressed behavior, the counselor became very quiet and withdrawn and appeared defeated. In response to the mood in the room and the child's growing disappointment, the counselor was vicariously experiencing the child's sadness.

Client Indicators

Verbal

In this case, the client directly informs the counselor of the over involvement.

Case Vignette

A counselor at an employment agency was very pleased with a client who had successfully completed a training course and was granted an interview for a prospective job. The counselor had met with the client on a regular basis and had formed a close working relationship that included regular meetings and telephone calls to ensure that the client was following through on his commitments. But when the counselor suggested that he drive the client to his job interview, the client politely refused his offer and stated that he was capable of getting to the interview on his own. Thrilled with the client's progress, the counselor forgot about the humble role he played in the client's life and began to erroneously inflate his importance.

Nonverbal

The client exhibits frustration, resentment, or anger, or prematurely terminates counseling.

Case Vignette

To assist a father and an adolescent son in resolving their differences regarding privileges, counselor suggested a conjoint interview. During the initial interview, the counselor asked the father to begin by explaining to his son his rationale for limiting privileges. As the father started to express his concerns about the poor decisions his son had made and his recent lack of confidence in his son, the counselor worried about the son's reaction and intimated that perhaps the father was being too harsh and judgmental. Feeling frustrated and undermined by the counselor, the father accused the counselor of siding with his son and left the interview prematurely.

Summary

The indicators discussed above, along with others, may suggest that counselors have transgressed the boundaries between themselves and clients. A careful examination or review of the therapeutic process can reveal repetitive patterns involving counselors and violations of boundaries. Such clinical deviations commonly occur around specific topics, themes, or transactional patterns that seem to engage both counselor and client in a systemic dance. By remaining unnecessarily central or by returning to this position prematurely, counselors may reinforce or avoid issues, which prolongs or interrupts client progress. The degree and timing of counselor participation becomes increasingly important during the course of treatment.

When clients seek a solution to a problem, counselors may find themselves at center stage with a customer eagerly requesting direction and guidance. To better understand counselor overinvolvement, it is important to determine how counselors assume the role of the central character in the counseling context when initially engaging clients. The misuse or abuse of this position, due to a lack of knowledge or awareness, can lead to counselor entanglement in client problems and with other systems involved in a client's life.

Assuming, utilizing, and relinquishing this central position needs to occur at strategic transition points during counseling. In other words, there will be times when counselors find themselves more involved in a client's story or situation than others. Gravitation toward a client's stories or dilemmas may be prompted by a counselor's personal issues or history. Counselors who work toward identifying and remaining aware of personal vulnerable points during self-supervision are better equipped to avoid emotional overinvolvement. Rather than conceptualizing therapy as two distinct subsystems, one that includes the counselor and another that includes the client, systems overlap should be acknowledged wherein counselors and clients share a degree of common ground that is constantly shifting as counseling proceeds. Penn (1982) referred to this circular process that connects counselors and clients as *co-evolutionary.*

The concepts of centrality and overinvolvement are distinguished by specific counselor behaviors. Counselors who are central often direct the flow of counseling. Despite this position, it is important that counselors can withdraw from this focal position without interrupting the overall interactional process. Counselors who effectively use their centrality appreciate the developmental process of counseling and their fluctuating position. On the other hand, when counselor maneuverability begins to diminish, for whatever reason, counselor overinvolvement usually follows. Rather than feeling a sense of therapeutic autonomy, overinvolved counselors frequently feel and appear to be part of the client system and experience the repercussions of this transgression.

After reviewing the literature pertaining to family therapist–client struggle, Butler and Bird (2000) reported the following:

> Research reviewed earlier informs therapists concerning risks for struggle associated with interjecting therapist expertise and hierarchy in the clinical narrative. These same findings may caution therapists concerning interposing themselves between spouses or family members and centralizing themselves in clinical interaction. (p. 133)

According to these authors, specific counselor behaviors such as teaching, interpretation, labeling, advice giving, and confrontation involve high levels of direct couple or family member interaction and prevent or disrupt couple or family interaction. These activities tend to be associated with hierarchy and counselor expertise and can contribute to the counselor-client struggle.

It is not uncommon for counselors to deliberately maintain a position close to the client. This therapeutic positioning is intentional, and may be especially useful during the initial phase of treatment, when counselors are attempting to engage clients and gather information about the presenting problem. This task can be arduous and demanding of the counselor's energy and attention. In order for clients to feel heard and understood, it becomes necessary for counselors to assume a very central position. Should a counselor assume a distant position and appear disinterested in a client's narrative, it is unlikely that counseling will proceed. Behaviors that place counselors at greater risk of overinvolvement or underinvolvement are discussed in more detail in Chapter 3.

☐ Cycle of Counselor-Client Conflict

Intrapersonal and interpersonal dynamics can inadvertently promote conflict and culminate in a traumatizing experience for clients and counselors. Counselor-client conflict can be the result of counselor emotional overinvolvement with clients and blatant counselor violations against clients (Edelwich & Brodsky, 1991; Heyward, 1993; Peterson, 1992; Strean, 1993). Counselors' negative assumptions about clients can impede the therapeutic process, creating an adversarial relationship in which the counselor and client are pitted against one another, which often lengthens treatment (O'Hanlon & Wilk, 1987). Framo (1985) and Andersen (1987, 1991) asserted that counselors can degrade clients through snide remarks, jokes, or hostile interpretations of their clients' behaviors. Unfortunately, a "we-they" dichotomy that is fueled by combative assumptions and language usually surfaces. The influence of a counselor's verbal and nonverbal expressions needs to be acknowledged and appreciated in order to promote a productive therapeutic experience (de Shazer, 1994; Efran, Lukens, & Lukens, 1990; Goolishian & Winderman, 1988).

☐ Complementary Coupling Behaviors

Complementary coupling behaviors provide a basis for understanding how conflict between counselors and clients can develop and spiral to various levels of intensity. For example, clients who perceive counselors becoming inpatient (e.g., completing sentences for the client, interrupting the client, or unilaterally changing the focus of the session) might become anxious and defensive (e.g., deciding to emotionally withdraw, suggesting that the counselor doesn't understand). In response to client defensiveness, counselors might become self-protective and, in turn, criticize clients. In describing this complementary coupling of negative behaviors, Coyne, Wortman, and Lehman (1988) wrote:

> With each exchange, the helper has invested more and more of his or her own esteem and well-being and interprets the partner's lack of progress in a highly personalized way. Having become involved, the helper has accepted some of the responsibility for a positive outcome and part of the blame if it is not achieved. (p. 317)

Accordingly, when counselors perceive themselves as having lost control of a session they may take action to correct the situation and restore their status and sense of competency. In doing so, they may project their personal shame and discomfort onto clients and hold clients responsible for their personal anguish. Pearlman and Saakvitne (1995) asserted that, "When a therapist struggles with shame or a sense of diminishment (internally or in front of her colleagues), she can take a therapeutic impasse personally and blame or become enraged at the client" (p. 271). The resulting anxiety and discomfort experienced by counselors and clients frequently eventuates into a vicious cycle wherein clients are perceived to be oppositional, ungrateful, or resistant (C. Anderson & Stewart, 1983; Marshall, 1982; Strean, 1990; Wachtel, 1982) and counselors are perceived to be unhelpful and ineffective. Grosch and Olsen (1994) commented that counselors may not be prepared for the lack of expressed appreciation from their clients:

> Constant giving in a one-way relationship, without feedback or perceived success, is hard on anybody. But some people apparently have a much more difficult time than others sustaining the unreciprocated attentiveness that is part of the psychotherapeutic relationship. We might speculate that these are people who go into helping primarily to gain gratitude, people with high need to be admired or people who depend on external praise to let them know they're headed in the right direction. Some people become therapists not so much to help people as to get people to like them. (p. 15)

As a result of the increased anxiety, the counseling system becomes mutually reactive and adversarial.

Counselor projection of blame onto clients for difficulties in the counseling relationship disregards the bi-directional nature of therapy. Kerr and Bowen (1988) elaborated:

> The emotional functioning of the patient in therapy, in other words, cannot be separated from the emotional functioning of the therapist. It is a system of interaction. Major problems arise when the therapist loses sight of his part in the process and responds to the patient's transference by diagnosing it as the patient's problem. (p. 111)

If left unresolved, the conflict between counselors and clients can fester and corrode efforts to interrupt and replace pathologizing interpersonal patterns in the relationship (Palmer, 1981). Often, participants in these relationships are unaware of how they are contributing to the perpetuation of the situation. Campbell, Draper, and Huffington (1991), for example, asserted that counselors sometimes blame clients for not telling them what they want to hear and formulate hypotheses about families, rather than considering their own contributions to the therapeutic impasse. This ignorance can be attributed to participants focusing on the possible meanings of specific behaviors rather than the overall interactional pattern. As a result, the dysfunctional pattern becomes further entrenched as counselors and clients feel emotionally wounded and resort to increased self-protectiveness.

☐ Epistemology and Counselor-Client Conflict

It has been suggested that counselors who adhere to a pragmatic empha- sis in counseling, based on a power epistemology (e.g., Allman, 1982; deShazer, 1982; Keeney & Sprenkle, 1982), may increase the likelihood of participating in conflictual relationships with clients. Similarly, practitioners who consider their work to be aesthetically based are also vulnerable (Hoffman, 1988). Counselors are all influenced by societal values that inform their particular theoretical beliefs. These values also influence personal perceptions and cognitions that trigger both emotional and physiological reactions. Counselor's values are influenced by several variables including their age, marital status, gender, and ethnic, religious, and sociocultural background (Baruth & Manning, 1999; Devore & Schlesinger, 1999; Green, 1999). Counselor reactions are often subtle—counselors may not even be aware of them. Counselor-client conflicts also seem to frequently involve practitioners who are attempting to master a specific model or intervention. Under such circumstances, counselors are more focused on theory and the mechanics of counseling than on the nuances that comprise the counseling relationship, particularly their own internal processes.

Despite the benefits of adhering to a specific model, counselors need to remain cognizant of their feelings and the range of behaviors that can influence clients. An unyielding adherence to a specific theoretical framework can produce rigidity and inflexibility, and contribute to an oppressive rather than liberating counseling encounter. For example, when there is a poor fit between particular clients and treatment approaches, both clients and counselors may experience some discomfort. Unfortunately, client discomfort may be misinterpreted by counselors as client ambivalence, uncooperativeness, or resistance. By remaining overly focused on a theoretical framework of a specific model, counselors may inadvertently overlook the more subtle interactions of counseling.

☐ Therapeutic Alliance and Collaboration

Over the past several years, clinicians advocating constructivist thinking in counseling practice (e.g., Franklin & Nurius, 1998; McNamee & Gergen,

1995; Sexton & Griffin, 1997) have encouraged helping professionals to form therapeutic alliances and closer associations with clients. While moving away from language and strategies espousing professional distance, they have emphasized the importance and influence inherent in a therapeutic alliance based on collaboration and respect. Although the social stage and client engagement are not new topics in the counseling literature (e.g., Haley, 1987, Minuchin, 1974), the aforementioned movement went beyond engagement strategies and involved a much deeper level of interaction and experience between counselors and clients.

In explicating their position, Goolishian and Winderman (1988) pointed to a new direction that went beyond the formalities of treatment and centered on perceptual and attitudinal changes in the counselor's approach with clients. They wrote:

> We have stated that we have moved away from the notion that therapists possess superior, private, privileged knowledge that allows them to diagnose the ontological reality of the system. Instead we moved in the direction of a collaborative problem definition that begins with the intersection of two phenomenological domains (a) from the therapist's position, it is our curiosity about the people with whom we are concerned; (b) from the client's position, it is their alarmed concern or objection to perceived experience, either cognitive or behavioral, which sets in motion the interaction between the individuals who are in communication about this alarmed objection. (p. 138)

Historically, throughout the counseling literature, there have been examples of language fostering distance between counselors and clients. In some instances, clients have been depicted in adversarial roles (Nichols, 1987). Warnings for counselors to avoid *family pull* or *induction*, for example, are well documented (Zupan, Babcock, & Morrissette, 1988). Counselors were explicitly cautioned to remain guarded from the client system. A result of such linear thinking and language was the dichotomization within the counseling relationship, as previously mentioned. Distance between counselors and clients ensued, with a competitive edge underlying interactions. Friendly client gestures were perceived as induction strategies designed to capture and trap counselors; client responses and behaviors were carefully scrutinized for hidden messages; and client apprehension was perceived as resistance and a struggle for power.

In addition to the language used, the traditional working and training environments along with methods employed by counselors, inadvertently created distance between themselves and clients. An obvious example is the one-way mirror: Although initially designed as a training tool (Cade & Cornwell, 1985; Haley, 1976), the mirror was often described as a safeguard against potentially dangerous situations. For example, it has been called a safe booth (Kassis & Matthews, 1987), a form of protection

(Landau-Stanton & Stanton, 1986), a filter (Nichols, 1984), and a boundary (Cornwell & Pearson, 1981). This protective barrier supposedly sheltered counselors from something that could be transmitted by clients. When described in these terms, counseling becomes akin to combat, with counselors and client as opponents. Further, the counselors situated behind the mirror were excluded from participation in the counseling system.

Critics of established counseling models began to forge new clinical directions. For example, deShazer (1985) suggested that adversarial terms such as "client resistance" be abandoned and a solution-focused approach based on client cooperation be adopted. White's (1990) model of externalizing problems called for counselors and clients to join forces in an endeavor to change problematic behavior patterns. Hoffman (1988) advocated self-disclosure and closer emotional proximity with clients. Rather than remaining guarded, she suggested a collaborative approach to problem solving wherein counselors introduced a personal element during the counseling process (Nichols, 1989). By doing so, they would be required to discard the *expert role*. Hoffman went so far as to suggest abolishment of the one-way mirror. She candidly stated:

> On the other side of the mirror, I was often dismayed to find myself part of an extremely competitive debate as different team members jockeyed among themselves to find the *bomb that would blow* [italics in original] the family system out of the water. There was a general feeling of being at war with the family and having to outmaneuver. (p. 121)

O'Hanlon and Wilk (1987) discussed the restrictiveness of traditional epistemological presuppositions in psychotherapy. In reference to the possible effect such suppositions can have on the counselor-client relationship, they wrote:

> In our view, these assumptions tend to lead to protracted treatment, to create barriers to results, and to create the context for an adversarial relationship between therapists and clients, in which therapist and client are pitted against one another. In our observations, of other therapists' work, it has been our impression that these assumptions often contribute to therapists' unwitting disrespect toward and suspicion of their clients. In our experience, operating from any, several, or all of these principles leads to frustration for both client and clinician. (p. 96)

As various worldviews of counseling evolved, new techniques designed to promote a closer counselor-client relationship were developed and explored. In describing elements of the reflecting team, for example, Andersen (1987) stated that he and his colleagues began to view themselves as merely participants in the therapeutic process and to consider clients as equals. The distinction drawn by Andersen regarding the role of counselors was significant. Rather than simply conceding that counselors were part of the counseling system (a concept that, of course, was not novel), Andersen (1987) spoke of counselors as being players during the course of treatment. He noted, "We no longer use a team break to unburden ourselves of tensions and personal feelings about the family we have been seeing by making funny jokes or disparaging remarks" (p. 427). Kassis and Matthews (1987) reported that many of their trainees, when working without the one-way mirror, experienced an increased emotional closeness with clients and consequently gained a better understanding of their fears and concerns. Apparently, this new understanding allowed the trainees to become more empathic and less reactive to clients, thus producing a better counselor-client relationship.

☐ Counselor Self-Disclosure

The idea of forming an emotionally close relationship with clients can certainly be an appealing objective. Feeling accepted, trusted, useful, and in sync with clients might be a tremendous motivational factor for counselors. What needs to be considered, however, are the reasons and consequences associated with developing such an alliance. Regardless of a counselor's clinical experience or the degree to which they self-disclose, the idea of counselor transparency in forming and strengthening a therapeutic relationship warrants careful attention.

The Self-Disclosure Continuum

The issue of counselor self-disclosure is a contentious, complex issue with a wide variety of opinions. Self-disclosures vary enormously in both content and purpose. For instance, some counselors may volunteer innocuous information regarding favorite restaurants or vacation spots, while others divulge substantial information regarding illness or sexual preference, and yet others use disclosure more judiciously and after assessing the needs of each client. Clinicians within the latter group assume a more moderate position (Bradmiller, 1978).

Proponents view disclosure as a transparency that allows clients to learn about counselor strengths and imperfections. Such transparency is considered necessary to remain honest and authentic. Bradmiller (1978), for example, noted that many authors have suggested that the sharing of knowledge about oneself reveals one's individuality and uniqueness, and it is "a gift of love, a demonstration of trust, and an invitation to be close" (p. 28).

At the other end of the continuum, there is the opinion that counselors need to remain opaque and anonymous in order for clients to work through their issues. It has been posited that counselors who share intimate information effectively block client transference and projections and are usurping their ability to heal. Also, disclosing counselors are perceived by some as contributing to a role reversal and using the counseling relationship to heal a personal vulnerability (Palombo, 1987).

Counselor Disclosure Styles

The manner in which disclosures occur also vary. For example, counselors may disclose information *spontaneously*, while others use disclosures *intentionally*. *Spontaneous* disclosures are considered involuntary and unpredictable, as exemplified below. These are not planned events but occur when an issue is triggered within the professional. It is generally accepted that spontaneous emotions might reflect unresolved issues within the professional and thus jeopardize the counseling process and/or relationship.

Case Vignette

Dr. Lewis, a psychologist, was asked to assess Cindy, who was referred to the university counseling center by a physician for academic-related problems. According to the intake form, Cindy was reporting irritability and an inability to concentrate, and was considering withdrawing from classes. Cindy's physician was concerned about possible depression.

During the first session, Dr. Lewis asked Cindy about her current circumstances and possible factors that might be contributing to her situation. Cindy reported starting the school year enthusiastically and experiencing success academically and socially. Recently, however, she was losing interest in her career goal and was unsure of what was important. Dr. Lewis became curious about Cindy's recent mood change and asked about her friends and social network. With great reservation and after prompting from Dr. Lewis, Cindy began to explain that after a heated argument, she and her boyfriend had decided to terminate their relationship. Cindy said that although she had felt exploited and mistreated in the relationship, she missed her boyfriend and was extremely lonely without him. She went on to describe how the evenings and weekends were especially painful.

During Cindy's story, and without warning, Dr. Lewis became tearful. Before Cindy could continue, Dr. Lewis interjected about how agonizing a lost love could be. He alluded to his recent divorce and how difficult it was to fill in the empty space. Cindy was surprised by Dr. Lewis' reaction and sat quietly as he tried to regain his composure.

Simon (1990) defined *intentional* disclosures as "verbal behavior through which therapists consciously and purposefully communicate ordinarily private information about themselves to their patients (p. 208).

Case Vignette

Beverly worked as a clinical social worker for a treatment foster care program. In addition to planning placements, she also conducted after-school group therapy for children who were in foster care. The groups were designed to provide children with a supportive context wherein they could discuss a variety of issues.

During one session, a youngster began to discuss how his previous physical abuse prohibited him from learning and behaving within the regular classroom. According to the youngster, his life was wrecked and there was no use in trying to improve his lot in life. After listening to the boy and considering his pain and sense of abandonment, Beverly revealed that she too had been physically abused as a child and placed in foster care. She further described how the abuse by her mother affected her self-esteem and how she began to feel worthless. Beverly proceeded to speak to the group about resiliency and the power of support and determination.

According to Simon (1990), counselor disclosure has been viewed as the antithesis of observer detachment. This statement implies that a closeness develops between self-disclosing counselors and their clients. Opposed to remaining neutral, disclosing counselors might volunteer personal information to introduce a degree of intimacy that will enhance the therapeutic relationship. Palombo (1987) remarked, "Self-disclosures made intentionally or unintentionally often have the effect of engendering greater closeness. These place the therapist in the position of opening the door to a level of intimacy that may take the process into totally uncharted regions" (p. 114).

Some professionals believe that disclosures are fundamental to the counseling process and that a mutual sharing of personal information serves to strengthen the therapeutic relationship. The premise upon which this argument is based is that clients and counselors need to relate to and identify with each other in order for a healing relationship to develop. Moreover, the reciprocity effect inherent in disclosures has been recognized (Jourard, 1964). In short, disclosure by one person leads to disclosure by another person.

Theoretical Orientation Influence

Simon (1990) contended that a decision to reveal information is usually determined by a theoretical orientation. High disclosures, for example, generally fall into the eclectic, humanistic, and existential categories. She further commented that counselors within these categories

viewed the therapeutic factors in their work as truth, love, communication, understanding oneself, and the human bond. The stance of friendliness and personal connectedness was consistent with their theoretical conception of quality psychotherapy and therapist self-disclosure was regarded as enhancing these factors." (p. 209)

☐ Client Responses to Counselor Disclosure and Overinvolvement

It can be hypothesized that clients are very sensitive to counselor change. Therefore, to protect clients from becoming confused or personalizing a sudden change in a counselor's disposition, counselors may inform their clients about their personal circumstances. Due to the potential impact (positive or negative) of counselor self-disclosure on the client system, it is imperative that counselors wisely determine the quality, quantity, and appropriateness of such disclosures. Depending on the client system, counselor disclosure might be received in different ways. For some, it might be perceived as genuineness on the part of counselors; on the other hand, it might evoke negative evaluations of the counselor's mental health or professional conduct.

While attempting to develop a close therapeutic relationship with clients, counselors can quickly find themselves overinvolved in treatment (Coyne et al., 1988; Zupan et al., 1988). Possible negative consequences stemming from counselor overinvolvement can affect both helping professionals and clients. Coyne et al. (1988) have done a superb job in providing an interactional perspective on the helper-helpee relationship and in discussing the various ramifications of emotional overinvolvement and miscarried helping.

Why, when, and how counselors decide to interact with clients is directly related to their epistemological base. Kottler (1991) suggested that to communicate warmth, authenticity, and humanness without diminishing authority and expertise, counselors should ask themselves several questions. These questions, provided in Table 2.1, would be ideal for counselors to consider during the self-supervision process.

Particular beliefs counselors hold regarding clients will affect their interactional style and the way in which they intervene in the counseling process. For example, viewing clients who enter counseling as basically needy, as opposed to competent; helpless, as opposed to capable; sick, as opposed to stuck will certainly have a bearing on the way in which counselors draw boundaries and conduct counseling. Counselors can either challenge clients to search for their own solutions or provide one for them. For example, counselors who believe that clients are unable to make appropriate appointments for themselves may overcompensate for this conception of a personal deficit, perhaps undermining what resources and

---
TABLE 2.1. Potential Self-Disclosure Questions

---
1. What do I hope this disclosure will accomplish?
2. Is there another way of making the same point?
3. What do I risk by not sharing myself?
4. To what extent am I attempting to meet my own needs?
5. Is this the right time?
6. How can I say this most concisely?
7. How will the client personalize what I share about myself?
8. How can I put the focus back on the client?

Taken from Kottler, J. (1995). Reprinted with permission by John Wiley & Sons, Inc.

confidence a client already possesses. Regarding counselor perspective and treatment impact, Woulff and Bross (1982) wrote:

> Another main source of therapist error can occur when therapists accept a patient statement of helplessness and hopelessness. Patients can be quite convincing in protesting that they are doing everything that has been suggested and that the problem is incurable. After many months of work with a family showing little change, the therapist may be tempted to agree with this myth. The therapist can become a helpless sympathizer rather than a proponent of change. (p. 8)

As counseling enters a new millenium, new perspectives on practice and the counselor-client system are becoming increasingly evident in the literature. Having grappled with various theoretical frameworks and strategies, counselors now appear to be seeking a closer, more egalitarian affiliation with clients when working toward change. This evolutionary shift is significant to the self-supervision process wherein counselors search for common ground and keys to solutions (deShazer, 1985). To many, this shift may signify a regression to old ways. This perception, however, may contain more falsehoods than truths. Although the originators of contemporary counseling models may be calling for a closer collaboration with clients and increased respect for the client system, the methods for achieving these ends are innovative and reflect new thinking in the counseling field.

☐ Conclusion

Embarking on a therapeutic relationship involves a blend of spontaneity, personal insight, and professional precision. Viewing the therapeutic relationship through a systemic lens allows counselors to appreciate the reciprocal nature of human interactions. During self-supervision, clinicians can remind themselves that counseling is not a one-sided affair. Counselors do not act upon clients, nor do clients act upon counselors. Instead, there are ongoing invitations from each side to participate in interactions.

The degree to which counselors participate in treatment is governed by several factors including past relationships in their family of origins, current life and professional circumstances, and their clinical training and experience. These factors will also dictate the degree of counselor disclosure. As discussed in this chapter, the issues of counselor centrality and disclosure are far from neat and tidy. Only after careful review do personal and clinical ramifications become apparent.

Although underreported in the counseling literature, the conflict and hostility that can erupt between professionals and clients deserves special consideration. As discussed in the following chapter, counselors bring a great deal into a counseling session. Their values, beliefs, and clinical preferences influence how they interact with clients.

☐ Review/Discussion Questions

1. Discuss the concept of counselor-client boundaries.
2. Identify some indicators of counselor overinvolvment.
3. Explain the cycle of conflict that can occur between counselors and clients.
4. What are some advantages and disadvantages of counselor self-disclosure?

3

Person-of-the-Counselor

To every therapy session we bring our human qualities and the experiences that have influenced us. In my judgment this human dimension is one of the most powerful determinants of the therapeutic encounter that we have with clients. If we hope as counselors to promote growth and change in our clients, we must be willing to promote growth in our own life.

—Gerald Corey, 1997

Contemporary helping professionals are much more active and involved with clients. No longer do professionals sit outside the client system. Rather, they state opinions, give advice, and become activists for clients. They pay careful attention to the human element in the counseling relationship. According to Aponte and Winter (1987), counselors are most effective when they use themselves for client and personal advancement. This statement emphasizes the reciprocal growth process within the counseling context and begins to draw a correlation between professional development and clinical effectiveness. As counselors learn more about personal strengths, needs, and limitations, they become better equipped to enter into the counseling process. Johnson (1995) remarked that counselors who acknowledge their limitations and are not intimidated by them may find that their skills are constantly expanding. On the other hand, counselors who do not admit limitations are likely to do harm, or at least fail to help. Simply said, counselors who are more self-aware may enjoy a better understanding of self in relation to clients. As aptly put by Hackney and Cormier (1996), "On the road to becoming an effective counselor, a

56

good starting place for most counselors is a healthy degree of introspection and self-exploration" (p. 15).

☐ Counselor-Client Parallel Growth Process

In addressing the person and practice of counselors, Aponte and Winter (1987) considered various aspects of a counselor's life including professional, collegial, and familial relationships. How these aspects converge and influence professionals is critical to the self-supervision process. Being oblivious to or ignoring how personal current (e.g., marital separation) and past (e.g., trauma, loss) life events can impact one's cognitive process and behavior may result in ineffective clinical work. Rober (1999) asserted that aspects of self are frequently neglected by counselors:

> There are a lot of possible reasons for this negligence: the things that are evoked in the therapist by his observations can be strange or bewildering, or they may, at least at first glance, not fit the theories or the experiences of the therapist, or they may be scary or shameful for the therapist or for the family, and so on. In these cases, therapists might dismiss these aspects of the self as unimportant, uninteresting, or irrelevant. (p. 216)

Being inattentive to, or ignoring, personal issues that effect treatment are missed chances at personal growth and, perhaps, improved service delivery. As will be discussed later, it is no easy feat to simultaneously focus on both self and clients. As counselors become engrossed in clients' captivating narratives and descriptions, they can lose sight of their position in the counseling context. As they gravitate to client stories, therapeutic boundaries shift and counselors can begin feeling overwhelmed, disoriented, or lost. The feelings experienced by such counselors are very real, originate from within, and accent the human element in counseling. Along these lines, Hartmann (1997) commented that counselors must be aware of how one's own boundaries shift due to stress, tiredness, sleep deprivation, and so forth.

In deconstructing the counseling process, Aponte and Winter (1987) reminded us that despite theoretical and technological advancements in the field of counseling, the counseling process can still be reduced to the interaction of people. They wrote, "In the psychotherapy session, the individual therapist utilizes his expertise and knowledge, as well as his personal life experiences and value system in order to engage with clients in ways that will improve the quality of the client's lives" (p. 85). Regardless of the treatment philosophy or approach, the self or the personhood of counselors is intimately involved in the helping relationship (Satir, 1987). Corey (1997) echoed this sentiment when stating that the current trend in counseling stresses the values and behavior of counselors. In short, although the counseling field has become more refined through research and innovative practice techniques, the person-of-the-counselor remains central but has a history of being underinvestigated (e.g., Norcross & Prochaska, 1986).

☐ Counselor Values, Assumptions, and Life Experiences

It is crucial for counselors to remember that regardless of advanced clinical training, degrees, or certificates, they continue to bring with them values and assumptions that will effect their work with clients. Understanding how history and present life circumstances can influence interactions with clients and treatment outcome is not always simple. Of course, only with experience is the connection made. Some counselors politely acknowledge this notion but place little value on its worth. Having secured formal training and an academic degree, these professionals assert that they have come to grips with their own issues and are fully aware of how their current circumstances can potentially effect their work. Counselors who ignore relevant clinical observations or events may be missing valuable growth and therapeutic opportunities. These individuals appear to choose a "wait and see" or "it won't happen to me" approach, and do not show an interest in ongoing self-exploration. In some situations, counselors are unaware of how their current and past life experiences solidify their values, beliefs, and behaviors. Working toward identifying and understanding the importance of life experiences in clinical practice is basic to the self-supervision process.

When training counselors, Aponte and Winter (1987) considered four areas of expertise that counselors should focus on to attain a positive therapeutic outcome: (a) external skills, (b) internal skills, (c) theoretical skills, and (d) collaborative skills. To summarize, external skills refer to the actual technical behavior of counselors; internal skills pertain to the personal integration of a counselor's own experiences when working with clients; theoretical skills involve the acquisition of a conceptual map that guides treatment; and collaborative skills refer to how counselors coordinate their efforts with other professionals. Of these areas of expertise outlined by Aponte and Winter, internal skills are central and, in fact, regulate a counselor's conceptualization, technical behavior, and collaborative abilities. In other words, without an understanding of self in the counseling process, counselors may be unsure of why they are employing various strategies or why they are becoming frustrated with clients. Even more fundamental, counselors may be unsure of why they have gravitated to the helping profession. When asked about their decision to become counselors, common responses included, "I just like people," "I want to make a difference in just one person's life," or "Someone was there for me and I want to be there for someone." These are noble intentions, but counselors are invited to think more deeply about why they have chosen a career in which they find themselves intimately involved in the lives of others. This point is not meant to insinuate that professionals should be able to explain precisely why they have chosen counseling as a career, but rather to encourage counselors to consider significant life events that have influenced their decision. Webb (1997) elaborated:

> Counselors should understand their own motivations in going into counseling and the likely risks attached to these motivations. Their needs, preferences and pattern in relation to distance and intimacy require exploring, as do their attitudes to their sexual functioning. Knowing their own symptoms of stress and burnout, and identifying the particular types of client they have difficulty helping, including emotional responses they experience towards these clients, are also important. (p. 183)

There is rarely just one factor that motivates one's interest in becoming a caregiver (Maslach, 1982). Kottler (1991), for example, outlined several factors including title and assumed role, power or control, intimacy, finances, narcissism, and personal growth. Fox (1987), writing about child caregivers, asserted that the failure of caregivers to acknowledge personal motives accounts for much of the punishment that occurs in lieu of nonpunitive discipline. Moreover, she wrote:

> It is not immature or unprofessional to admit our needs; rather, I believe it is unprofessional not to admit our needs. If we keep them out of our awareness they will surely be expressed in ways that are harmful to those in our care; consequently we will be unsatisfied. We must learn to acknowledge and address our feelings in order to avoid blaming and punishing the kids for not meeting our needs. (p. 45)

It is crucial that counselors understand their own limits through self-study. According to Thorne and Dryden (1991), unaware counselors who lead unexamined lives are likely to be a liability rather than an asset.

Although it sounds reasonable in theory, the process of introspection through self-reflection can be a challenging endeavor that involves discovery of unknown psychological terrain. Aponte (1994a) elaborated on the need for counselors to identify and explore personal issues that can potentially effect their work. As noted earlier, he encouraged vulnerability, discipline, and freedom within clinical relationships. In short, the person/practice model helps counselors to (a) understand and conceptualize issues from their lives, (b) gain mastery over their personal issues, and (c) learn to use the self during their interactions with clients. According to Aponte, "If therapists are able to see and feel the pain of their own experiences and to accept the contradiction and inconsistencies of their attitudes towards others, that will help them deal with similar feelings in the clients" (p. 155). He further notes that helping professionals "need to see how their experiences help and hurt them in order to understand their client's lives" (p. 156). Needless to say, self-reflection is fundamental to learning about oneself; it is discussed in greater detail in Chapter 4.

☐ Person/Practice Model

Within the Person/Practice Model described by Aponte (1994a), trainees seek to do the following:

1. Understand and conceptualize issues from their lives by
   (a) identifying and interpreting themes in their histories and current relationships through their genograms and personal family sessions;
   (b) accessing emotionally their own personal struggles, past and present;
   (c) articulating templates for themselves for how they have succeeded and failed with their personal and family issues;
   (d) making explicit for themselves personal values, philosophy, and social factors that describe their lives and affect their therapy.
2. Gain mastery over their personal issues through
   (a) taking into personal therapy unresolved issues, especially those experienced in the professional context;
   (b) learning to think about, feel, and live with unresolved issues in order to facilitate working with them in therapy;
   (c) pursuing limited understanding, resolution, and management of their issues through their clinical practice.
3. Learn to use themselves in therapy by
   (a) developing the capacity for personal intimacy, mutuality, and commitment with clients inside professional boundaries;
   (b) discovering their clients in themselves and themselves in their clients through empathy;
   (c) differentiating self from their clients within the shared experience of the therapy process;
   (d) developing the skill to work with the connections between their own and clients' values and personal philosophy;
   (e) integrating their personal work with a professional model of therapy to achieve theoretical and practical congruity of the use of self in their therapy.

☐ Conversations with Self

Rober (1999) drew a distinction between the *self of the therapist* and the *role of the counselor.* In his view, the self of the therapist refers to "the experiencing process of the therapist as a human being and a participant in the conversation" (p. 214). The experiencing process of counselors includes their feelings, intuitions, fears, images, ideas, and so forth. The role of the therapist refers to "the therapist as a professional whose task it is to facilitate the conversation" (p. 214). As Rober pointed out, although possessing their own observations and interpretations, counselors filter what and how they respond when interacting with clients. More specifically, counselors monitor their self-talk to promote a healing conversation. He noted that counselors maintain an inner dialogue, which is the starting point of their therapeutic questions.

As counselors listen to clients, they are simultaneously formulating responses and additional questions. It can be said, of course, that this process occurs in all conversations, therapeutic or casual. The major difference between therapeutic and casual questions or responses is the context. Professionals do not have the luxury of responding in a casual way. Clients expect counselors to listen intently and respond accordingly. Counselors do not have the freedom to drift in and out of therapeutic conversations. Instead, they are expected to remain focused and attentive to client subtleties and nuances. This task becomes even more challenging as the client system increases in number or when presenting problems are especially meaningful or anxiety provoking for counselors.

Rober (1999) contended that, "The thoughts, ideas, prejudices, and images of the therapist are opportunities to initiate dialogue on the condition that they are offered in such a way that conversation is continued rather than closed" (p. 213). In other words, one idea should not monopolize the counselor's inner conversation, and his or her thinking should remain flexible. More importantly, counselors need to carefully consider the emotions that are invoked in them based on their observations and interpretations.

In explicating counselor inner conversations, Rober (1999) reported that:

1. The inner conversation is a conversation between two aspects of the person of the therapist, namely, the self of the therapist and the role of the therapist.
2. The inner conversation is a negotiation between self and the role of the therapist.
3. The negotiation is about what aspects of the self can be used to open

space for the not-yet-said in the outer conversation, and in what way these aspects can be used.

☐ A Family-of-Origin Focus

In addition to Aponte and Winter's (1987) work, McDaniel and Landau-Stanton (1991) designed a family-of-origin seminar for counselors. This elective graduate course is distinct from clinical work; it reviews the family-of-origin literature and provides trainees with opportunities to present information regarding their families of origin to the seminar participants. The information that is shared by participants is based on their own perceptions as well as conversations with other family members. Once the information has been gathered, participants develop a summary paper that discusses their findings.

   McDaniel and Landau-Stanton (1991) contended that a family-of-origin seminar serves a dual purpose of enhancing participant cohesion and providing invaluable information about events that can trigger counselor reactions. In discussing the potential effect of family-of-origin issues on counselors, these authors remarked, "The most telling signs of trainee stress we have come to call *The Family-of-Origin Freeze* [italics in original]. Here a trainee is conducting a session in a rather routine way and, seemingly abruptly, becomes rigid, sometimes pale, and begins to flounder" (p. 464). These authors noted that symptoms indicating that a client problem may be stimulating unresolved personal issues for counselors might include an inability to track a particular clinical problem, changing the subject, and forgetting to inquire about clinical tasks. Recognizing that a particular client problem stimulates unresolved personal issues can be a tremendous learning opportunity for counselors. The task for counselors, of course, is to link client problems with unresolved personal issues. This will entail the process of tracking a problem or theme throughout one's life.

☐ Transparency and Competency

Helping professionals might be hesitant to open their lives up to colleagues. Although they would like to share a personal problem (e.g., a chemical addiction, loneliness, financial debt), they wonder if their competency will be called into question or whether their peers will reject them. Rather than risk the consequences, they remain quiet, work in isolation, and miss out on opportunities to grow. This response may be safer for the professional, but, client service might well suffer. In describing the human side of counselors, Kottler and Hazler (1997) remarked:

> Few of us are as healthy as we appear to others, or even as we would like to be. There is a dark side to each of us, a part we keep hidden from view. Late at night when we are unable to sleep, or at other times when we are daydreaming, we are haunted by unresolved issues of our past, by things we have done for which we feel regret or shame, by our secrets long buried, by our weaknesses, our failures, and our imperfections. This is how human beings are, even when they are therapists. (p. 187)

Obviously, work situations that discourage disclosure and trust among colleagues contradict the basic core conditions of the helping profession. In other words, one would expect helping professionals to applaud a colleague's honesty and support his or her effort to heal. After all, counselors encourage honesty from and purport positive regard for clients. Surely these same principles can be extended to colleagues. Perhaps Rogers (quoted in Baldwin, 1987) said it best:

> The therapist needs to recognize very clearly that he or she is an imperfect person with flaws which make him vulnerable. I think only as long as the therapist views himself as imperfect and flawed that he can see himself as helping another person. Some people who call themselves therapists are not helpers, because they are too busy defending themselves. (p. 51)

There is no shame in working toward increased self-understanding. There may be times during self-supervision when a professional could personally benefit from counseling. Professionals who realize the need for outside expertise and support are fortunate and should not waste their time doubting their abilities or feeling shameful.

Kane (1995) remarked that although some counselor education programs recommend or require students to participate in individual or group therapy for personal growth, these programs fail to provide a clear focus on family-of-origin work. She further proposed that counselor education programs should provide opportunities for students to review relationships and issues related to their families of origin. To formalize this process, it was recommended that counselor education programs institute family-of-origin work in the academic curriculum. Corey (1997) reiterated:

> Although supervision with a personal focus on the counselor as a person may not be available in some educational and professional settings, it is essential that practitioners learn how to ask for supervision that involves self-review and the care of the counselor as well as supervision that focuses largely on case management or the dynamics of dealing with clients. (p. 21)

As with so many other issues in the counseling profession, not everyone agrees with the need to focus on the interfacing of counselor issues and treatment. While some strongly insist on a journey of self-discovery, others consider this exercise unnecessary.

☐ Models for Self-Exploration

There are a number of models available to counselors who are interested in self-exploration. Suggestions on how to use genograms, timelines, family autobiographies, and journaling have been discussed in the literature. The purpose of each model is briefly described below.

Genograms

Genograms are designed to graphically display multiple generations of a family and to increase awareness and sensitivity to intergenerational patterns. McGoldrick and Gerson (1985) described a genogram as a format for drawing a family tree that recorded information about family members and their relationships over at least three generations (e.g., siblings, parents, and grandparents). These authors noted that there was a loose consensus regarding what information needed to be collected to develop a genogram but that there was no single right way to construct this symbolic diagram. Genogram construction will vary depending on the individual needs of counselors and can be very useful in synthesizing information regarding their families of origin (Braverman, 1984). Lewis (1989) stated that three levels of family information are captured in a genogram including

> a) the basic structure, which includes who is in the family and the biological and legal relationships between members; b) demographic data such as births, deaths, marriages, as well as factual and mythical data about illnesses, personality, and behavior and c) relationships between people, such as enmeshment, disengagement, conflict, alliances. (p. 170)

Genograms can augment information that is gathered and allows counselors to graphically map out patterns in their own families of origin. The purpose in identifying patterns, of course, is to ensure that counselors do not replicate problematic patterns when treating clients. For example, one counselor, who also volunteers as a referee in youth sports, recently joked about the role he played as peacemaker between his parents. He wondered out loud if he also assumed the role of peacemaker in his social life and when working with clients.

Braverman (1984) used genograms in training counselors and psychiatric residents. She started the process by focusing on a counselor's description of his or her family and then moved to a description of a client family. Her focus was on helping professionals make important connections between themselves and their clients. In essence, there is a parallel search wherein counselors and clients attempt to discover family-of-origin patterns and themes.

Braverman (1984) made several recommendations to ensure that family-of-origin work remained a training resource and did not become therapy, as illustrated in Table 3.1. The teacher must have some time available after the session to deal with any unforeseen problem that might arise for the student presenter or the group.

There is variation in the design (e.g., Lewis, 1989) and use (e.g., Sproul & Gallagher, 1982) of genograms. For example, in terms of counselor development, Hardy and Laszloffy (1995) suggested that the cultural genogram can be used to enhance the growth of culturally competent counselors. They wrote, "The cultural genogram is a practical instrument for assisting trainees in becoming more familiar with their culturally constructed realities" (p. 236). They further reported that the cultural genogram has the potential to heighten counselor awareness of their cultural biases and "the numerous ways in which these are deeply embedded in the cultural genogram process" (p. 236).

Titelman's (1992) book, *The Therapist's Own Family: Toward a Differentiation of Self*, was devoted to helping professionals become more responsible in relationship to their own families. He suggested that

> Working toward becoming a more responsible and differentiated individual in one's own family provides an avenue for lessening tendencies to become overinvolved with one's clinical families, and it helps the family thera-

---

TABLE 3.1. Suggested Counselor Family-of-Origin Work Guidelines

1. The purpose should be clear and case related.
2. There must be a high level of trust and respect in the group for each other and the teacher.
3. Focus should be on the student's relationship to his family of origin and not his family of procreation.
4. It should be time limited so that the focus can remain on training and not on therapy.
5. Motivation is higher if the request for family-of-origin work comes from the students, rather than being imposed by the teacher.

Baverman, copyright 1984 in Family of Origin Applications in Clinical Supervision. Reprinted with permission of The Haworth Press.

pist avoid emotional *burn-out* [italics in original] a common occupational hazard for psychotherapists. (p. 4)

In essence, the purpose of family-of-origin exercises and genograms is to better understand the interlocking process that exists between counselors, their families of origin's, and their work with clients. The focus is on understanding oneself in the counseling context. For instance, it has been suggested that most psychotherapists and family therapists show a propensity to become overinvolved and overresponsible in their clinical work (Titelman, 1992). Based on this assumption, it would make sense for counselors to explore whether they feel anxious or obligated to make things right for clients.

Case Vignette

The Morris family was referred to Frank, who worked at a local cancer institute, for family counseling. The family consisted of Mr. Morris, who was a university professor; Mrs. Morris who was a teacher; and their three children, Matthew, Alana, and Samuel. Mrs. Morris' mother was diagnosed with terminal cancer and her husband wanted to ensure that he and his children were providing his wife with ample support. Mr. Morris was from a different culture and realized that his view of the death process differed from his wife.

Following the completion of intake information, Frank began to formulate a family genogram. The family was intrigued with the process and freely volunteered information. As he asked questions about Mr. and Mrs. Morris' families of origin, Mrs. Morris became very tearful. As Mrs. Morris wept, her husband remained quiet and made no physical attempt to console his wife. The children glanced over at their mother, but did not appear worried about her emotional disposition.

As Mrs. Morris continued to share thoughts about her mother, Frank became visibly uncomfortable and asked Mrs. Morris why her husband was not attending to her obvious needs. As he began to describe the difference in affective states between Mr. and Mrs. Morris, Frank took the liberty of providing Mrs. Morris with a tissue. Taken aback by his query, Mrs. Morris informed Frank that, in fact, her husband was very sensitive to her needs and was providing her with agreed-upon space to express herself. There was an obvious agitation in Mrs. Morris's response and Mr. Morris began to defend himself by explaining his position. Although the interview ended on a cordial note, the Morris family decided against returning to see Frank. During a consumer survey telephone call, Mrs. Morris stated that she disliked the way that her husband was treated and was no longer interested in counseling.

The above example is designed to demonstrate counselor reactivity and a possible implication associated with such behavior. Unaware that he was reacting to his own anxiety regarding Mrs. Morris's sadness, Frank became overly concerned and assumed a great deal about the couple's relationship. Although unintended, Frank's reaction was perceived as insulting and resulted in premature client termination.

Over- and Underfunctioning Counselors

Lawson and Gaushell (1988) describe the *overfunctioner* and the *underfunctioner* as two common patterns of triangulation in the family of origin that can be reenacted in later relationships. Both styles are used to avoid or reduce counselor anxiety. Overfunctioners, for example, tend to take charge of situations or assume a nurturing role. Underfunctioners, on the other hand, assume a position of weakness and invite others to take care of them. Lawson and Gaushell suggested that counselors who react inappropriately to anxiety-producing situations in treatment often assume one of these styles. Possible consequences of such behavior include the dampening or discouragement of client emotions or responses to accommodate counselor comfort.

In the case vignette above, Frank should consider a few important questions in order to avoid similar situations from occurring, including: Why did he become so anxious when Mrs. Morris began to cry? What did her emotions trigger in him? What did her tears symbolize for Frank? Why did he quickly judge Mr. Morris and become critical of him? What did Mr. Morris's behavior symbolize for Frank?

Counselor Anxiety and Emotional Proximity in Counseling

The emotional proximity between counselors and clients is governed by the level of anxiety within their relationship. For instance, if a client has a history of self-mutilation behaviors and the counselor responds anxiously in a protective manner, emotional space is likely to decrease and interpersonal boundaries to blur. The degree of counselors' reactivity can directly effect the level of their efforts to help and can paradoxically get in the way, particularly when efforts to help are incongruent with a client's personal plan. The disparity between caregiver and client needs can threaten the counseling relationship. Frequently, as counselors desperately try to help clients, clients begin to assume a complementary position as a way of creating emotional distance. In response, counselors become frustrated, escalate the transaction, and further pursue the client, who, in turn, becomes increasingly withdrawn and disinterested. Pearlman and Saakvitne (1995) remarked:

> Therapists can become injurious in the context of frustrated rescue fantasies, when they believe they have or should have more power over a client's process or progress than they can possibly have. When a rescue fantasy is fueled by a need for control, by a narcissistic need to be revered as a competent, powerful therapist, or by a need to be seen by one's colleagues as effective, a therapist can get into a power struggle with the client that centers more on the therapist's needs than the client's. (p. 271)

During such overfunction/underfunction reciprocity, the confidence level of the counselor is affected, resulting in a sense of powerlessness and defeat. Such interpersonal intensity can be fueled by counselor overidentification and is related to unresolved family-of-origin roles that continue to be played out.

Counselors may be unaware of their own needs, personal level of differentiation, and propensity toward overinvolvement and fusion. By underestimating the influence of intergenerational patterns, the focus centers solely on clients. As a result, the cognitive and behavioral processes of counselors in relation to clients is overlooked. Understanding their level of counselor differentiation within their families of origin is critical, in that a lower level of differentiation promotes enmeshment and a higher level of differentiation promotes interpersonal boundaries (Kerr & Bowen, 1988). Therefore, with a low base level of counselor differentiation, the prospect of any disruption to the emotional equilibrium of the counseling relationship can produce a high level of anxiety, interactional conflict, and eventual relationship deterioration. Kerr and Bowen wrote, "During high anxiety periods, human beings strive for oneness through efforts to think and act alike. It is ironic that this striving for sameness increases the likelihood that a group will become fragmented into subgroups" (p. 121).

Personal Timelines

In addition to genograms, counselors can work toward developing a personal timeline. Stanton (1992) described a method to quickly and graphically clarify the relationship between life cycle events and the onset of problems. This process is uncomplicated and involves laterally organizing nodal events and then corresponding these events with specific points in time. Timelines can assist counselors in identifying significant events that have effected, and perhaps continue to effect, their lives and work. Events that were disruptive and consequential to counselors may be of special interest. Stanton reported that there was no limit to the kinds of nodal events that can be highlighted, which usually included key births, deaths, marriages, chronic illnesses, transitions, work successes or failures, financial setbacks, and relocations.

The primary purpose of the timeline is to evoke questions and hypotheses in a counselor's mind regarding one's family of origin. Since Stanton (1992) discussed Type S and Type G structural timelines in great detail, they will be summarized here. Briefly, the *Type S timeline* is derived from the theory underlying Minuchin's (1974) structural family therapy approach. This type of timeline plots a number of structural maps along the timeline. Each map is pegged to nodal points where significant changes have occurred for a counselor. For example, during the long-term illness of a parent, a family's structure might have temporarily shifted and a counselor might have taken on parental responsibilities. Visualizing how he or she moved from the position of the oldest child into a parentified role may be useful information for a counselor who finds himself or herself assuming excessive responsibility.

The *Type G timeline* originates from the genogram and incorporates biological and legal relationships across generations. It also includes information on family history, demographics, personality characteristics, and various emotional, behavioral, and medical problems. Symbols are used to indicate structural variables such as closeness, conflicts, and emotional cutoffs.

According to Stanton (1992), both timeline models have strengths and weakness. Advantages of the Type G model, for example, are its completeness and sensitivity to multigenerational patterns. A disadvantage, however, is that it fails to reflect a family's hierarchy or interactional structure. An obvious limitation to the Type G model is the actual room needed in order to place extensive genogram information with each timeline event. Nevertheless, counselors who are interested in pursuing a detailed investigation of their families of origin may opt to integrate the strengths of each model.

Case Vignette

Kevin, who attended middle school, was referred to the school counselor, Mrs. Peters. Kevin was a good student who participated in school activities and was well liked by his peers. To his teachers' surprise, Kevin was beginning to withdraw from his peers and demonstrate a lack of interest in extracurricular activities.

During their initial meeting, Mrs. Peters praised Kevin for his academic and social behavior and candidly expressed the concerns of the teachers. Kevin freely agreed with Mrs. Peters and began to appear downcast. In response to Kevin, Mrs. Peters began to query Kevin about school-related issues that might have contributed to Kevin's emotional and physical withdrawal. With some reluctance, Kevin informed Mrs. Peters that his father had accepted a new job in a different city. As Kevin shared the circumstances with Mrs. Peters, his voice and facial expressions spoke volumes about his sadness. Having already moved several times to accommodate his father, Kevin was disappointed that he would have to once again pull up roots. As Mrs. Peters listened to Kevin, she found herself becoming upset, angry, and almost unable to respond to Kevin. The fact was that Kevin's circumstances reflected her own childhood. She had felt shuffled from city to city, unable to develop long-term relationships with friends. Only as she was driving home did Mrs. Peters begin to reflect on how she had begun to speak about Kevin's father in a derogatory fashion (e.g., self-centered, unfeeling) during the meeting, as well as on the ramifications of this behavior.

This vignette exemplifies how nodal events can influence the behaviors of counselors. In this particular case, the counselor had unresolved issues around fathers who appeared insensitive to the needs of their children. Although Mrs. Peters had not met Kevin's father and was not privy to the family's circumstances, she quickly generalized and labeled this man as callous. While speaking with Kevin, Mrs. Peters recalled how her father would spontaneously announce another family move to alleviate his boredom. Because her father was very adamant about the need to relocate, there would be no family discussion or debate.

As Mrs. Peters remembered those difficult times, she began to reexperience feelings of being discounted and cheated. Only after thinking about what had transpired between herself and Kevin did Mrs. Peters begin to realize how her personal history was coloring her work with Kevin.

Autobiographies

Written, audiotaped, or videotaped autobiographies have proven to be a useful tool for assisting counselors in the self-exploration process through the articulation of thoughts and actions. Autobiographies should not be confused with the journaling process, which is discussed in further detail below.

The purpose of the autobiography is to allow counselors to examine the influence of the intrapersonal and interpersonal dynamics within their families of origin on their current functioning. In advocating autobiographies to promote counselor personal growth, Lawson and Gaushell (1988) focused on the concepts of individuation and triangulation in the family of origin. In their opinion, "counselors' effectiveness is significantly increased by their ability to deal effectively with their own personal and interpersonal issues that might otherwise inhibit their emotional or psychological growth and development" (p. 162).

An obvious advantage of recording and securing an autobiography is that information can be retrieved at later dates. Some counselors value the opportunity to return to an earlier stage of their development to witness growth and change in different areas. In particular, counselors are generally surprised with how their values have changed over time. With age, clinical and personal experience, the influence of intimate relationships and parenthood, personal values and beliefs that were once indelible gradually shift—sometimes to a surprising degree!

Although documented autobiographies may be more common and well known, autobiographical audio- and videotapes may be appealing to professionals who dislike writing or find writing to be inconvenient. Winslade, Monk, and Drewery (1997), for example, described working toward grounding counselors in their own lives so that they could begin to understand how their beliefs and views contribute to the therapeutic relationship. To achieve this goal, they asked counselors to

> write a personal autobiography that focuses on the impact of the various discourses they have encountered on the sense of self that they have assumed as their own. Specifically they are asked to identify their positioning in dominant discourses that relate to gender, class, sexual orientation, and ethnicity. (p. 233)

According to Winslade et al., individuals who later processed their information found the experience wrenching and very enlightening regarding issues that were generally taken for granted.

Though the process may appear straightforward, many counselors have underlined the inherent challenge of reflecting upon oneself. Gibson and Mitchell (1999) commented that, "The autobiography lets a person express what has been important in his or her life, to emphasize likes and dislikes, identify values, describe interests and aspirations, acknowledge successes and failures, and recall meaningful personal relationships" (p. 282). Through the autobiographic exercise counselors can begin to make connections that are important when working with clients. The degree to which professionals can express themselves, however, will hinge on their readiness and maturity (Gibson & Mitchell, 1999).

The following reflective questions can help professionals to begin the self-exploration process.

1. What do you find interesting/disinteresting about this case?
2. What personal attributes may help or hinder your work with clients?
3. What values influence your work with this client?

Professionals are also invited to deviate from the preformulated questions and to create questions that are more personally meaningful and appropriate. Of course, some professionals may initially be confused or annoyed with what appears to be a simplistic and/or meaningless exercise. In their view, focus should be placed on the needs of clients and problem solving. In addressing a limitation of the autobiographical exercise, Gibson and Mitchell (1999) wrote,

> many people may find writing an autobiography a chore; thus, it will become a brief, bleak, and usually boring document that contributes little to a better understanding of the writer. The author's writing ability as well as the conditions under which it is written will influence the autobiography's potential usefulness. (p. 284)

Irving and Williams (1995) further commented that some counselors frown upon a critical analysis of ideas and assumptions that guide practice and consider it a form of intellectualization.

Finally, a professional's ability to recall significant events must be taken into consideration. For professionals who are unable to recall significant events upon which to reflect and connect to present circumstances, the autobiography may be meaningless.

Following completion of their autobiography, many professionals may be surprised to learn how their own personal history continues to influence their thinking processes and behaviors. One counselor reflected on the childhood anger she experienced toward her mother for "putting up with" her father's verbal and physical abuse. While completing her autobiography, she began to gain a better understanding of why she was appalled at clients who returned to abusive relationships. Other professionals share their realization that issues (e.g., eating disorders, substance abuse, addictions, intimate violence) that they thought were resolved were in fact simply being avoided or repressed. Providing ample time for professionals to discuss what they have discovered during discussions is critical to the transformation process. While sharing their findings, colleagues provide support and often reciprocate through personal narratives.

Supervisors who choose to utilize autobiographies as a training tool are encouraged to continually remind students that appropriate clinical services are available to them should they need to process their emotions. From a professional and ethical perspective, supervisors are also encouraged to inform students about the potential risks and repercussions associated with the assignment. As McDaniel and Landau-Stanton (1991) pointed out, the process of having counselors focus on the interface between their professional roles and their personal lives can stimulate strong feelings and lead to powerful and unexpected experiences. Thorne and Dryden (1991) elaborated:

> Some of these developments are likely to be disturbing and disorienting with the result that almost all trainees at some stage of their training are likely to experience periods of distress or bewilderment and may even at times become subject to incapacitating anxiety or depression. Notoriously, too, relationships with spouses and other family members are liable to undergo considerable upheaval or even to flounder altogether. (p. 4)

Students should be continually reminded that issues may emerge as they complete their autobiographies. Moreover, rather than avoiding these issues, students can be encouraged to reflect on their meaning and to consider how their clinical work is shaped by these experiences.

Audiotapes

When reviewing their audiotapes, professionals should pay special attention to accentuation and voice tone as they broach certain topics, issues, or circumstances. The influx of one's voice may indicate the need to consider feelings and emotions that are associated with a specific event or topic. Voice fluctuation may be out of the counselor's awareness until he or she has the opportunity to actually listen to himself or herself. This learning approach can be particularly helpful to counselors who struggle with specific presenting problems or clients.

Case Vignette

Karen, who worked as an agency counselor, admittedly struggled with clients who appeared to be physically forceful with their children. In addition to avoiding these cases at the weekly intake meeting, she found herself speaking in a derogatory fashion about such prospective clients. At the suggestion of a colleague, she agreed to explore her position and opinions during an audiotaped conversation.

During the conversation, the counselor described how children should feel wanted and protected. She also stated that parents should be grateful for having the honor of raising children. Karen emphasized that not all couples are able to have children and that those who are should appreciate what they have. Following the conversation, Karen expressed gratitude to her colleague for allowing her to further explore her feelings about such parents. Despite the opportunity to delve into the issue, however, nothing immediate seemed to change for Karen.

A few weeks following the conversation, Karen became curious and decided to review the audiotape. As she listened to her words and expressions, Karen began to think about her own struggles to have children. Listening to herself speak, Karen became overwhelmed with the resentment she experienced toward parents who appeared to mistreat their children. Feeling shameful, she began to realize that her own issues were influencing her work, but she was still unsure of how to correct the situation.

Videotapes

Videotape offers another opportunity to engage in the self-exploration process. This technique was observed during a professional development forum among counselors at a family therapy institute in the American Northwest. The process included colleagues sitting together and asking a volunteer group member questions about his or her earlier life, how he or she pursued a career in counseling, what life events were significant, how these events effected his or her work, and so forth. The conversation was casual, humorous, and, at times, solemn. Following the conversation, the colleague who shared his or her experiences would retrieve the tape for further reflection and possible discussion.

An advantage of the videotape is that counselors can observe their nonverbal behaviors as they discuss topics that are meaningful and emotionally significant. Such a review also provides counselors with an idea of what it might be like for clients who observe their nonverbal reactions. It has been theorized that clients are very perceptive of counselor reactions and tend to avoid issues that might disturb the professional. Although noble, this avoidance may restrict what issues a client can raise with the counselor.

Journaling

Professionals who prefer independent learning may find that journaling is an effective way to identify and track issues that arise. During or immediately following an interview, counselors can record their reactions to specific counseling situations that can later be processed individually or with others. By tracking events and reactions, counselors can begin to notice and address patterns in their work. Winslade, Monk, and Drewery (1997) further suggested that "students keep a journal in which they are free to write in an informal, provisional way of the thoughts they are having about their work and the connections they are building between practice and theory" (p. 234).

Stickel and Trimmer (1994) suggested that counselors use journals to gather information needed to probe personal thought processes that influence their decisions and actions. These authors suggested that journals can be used in either structured or unstructured forms and are useful in teaching principles of counselor reflectivity. Once experiences have been recorded, they can later be reviewed for underlying values and assumptions. To augment the reflective process, the utilization of a reflective model developed by Symth (1989) was encouraged. The stages are defined by a series of questions:

1. Describing: What do I do?
2. Informing: What does this mean?
3. Confronting: How did I come to be like this?
4. Reconstructing: How might I do things differently?

Arnold and Boggs (1995) provided valuable reflective journal guidelines for critical thinking about important incidents in practice. Reflective journaling, as described in Figure 3.1, is a process that can be used once or over a period of time.

☐ Ethical Considerations

Within group settings, confidentiality is central to participant disclosure and discussions. Due to the nature of issues, confidentiality must be continually stressed and maintained.

Purpose
The capacity to examine one's actions, thoughts, and feelings about professional practice is of particular significance in the development of professional attitudes. Reflective journals allow students to raise important questions, reflect on activities and progress, and consider new approaches and resources.

Procedure
1. Your first journal entry should be a short narrative reflecting on the persons, circumstances, situations, and values that drew you to consider nursing as a profession.
2. In subsequent weeks, or as a one-time learning experience, your journal entry should focus on your educational experience and address the following questions:
   • What was the most significant experience I had this week? The experience can be an incident, an encounter, or a discovery about self, client, or nursing.
   • What questions did it raise for me personally? As a professional?
   • How could I use what I learned from this experience in my nursing practice?

FIGURE 3.1. Guidelines for Reflective Journaling. Adapted from Arnold and Boggs (1995).

Prior to advocating counselor self-exploration and possible disclosure, ethical considerations surrounding this practice need to be acknowledged. Open discussions are opportunities for counselors to gradually experience a sense of vulnerability (not uncommon to clients) while understanding how their own issues can enhance or hinder interactions with clients and colleagues.

☐ Conclusion

Central to the self-supervision process is the process of self-exploration and self-discovery. As professionals go about helping others, they can also work toward gaining a fundamental understanding of self.

Several models are available to help counselors identify past and present personal behavioral patterns. A focus on personal histories and genograms can provide counselors with clues regarding how family interactional and relational patterns effect their current relationship with clients and colleagues. The models of self-discovery can be used independently or in combination with one another. For example, counselors have found the integration of genograms, timelines, and autobiographies to be useful.

When traveling in uncharted territory, there are risks involved and the potential for unexpected surprises. The self-exploration journey is no exception. Consequently, counselors would be wise to create a safety net of people who are willing to support them and share both pleasant and difficult moments. Professionals who are interested in beginning the self-exploration process within a group context must be mindful of confidentiality issues. There may also be times when counselors will need to seek assistance from objective professionals. Rather than perceive this need as a weakness or flaw, counselors are encouraged to take the opportunity to learn more about themselves.

☐ Review/Discussion Questions

1. Why is counselor self-exploration fundamentally important?
2. Describe and provide examples of over- and underfunctioning counselors.
3. List and describe several models of counselor self-exploration.

4
CHAPTER

Reflectivity: The Essence of Self-Supervision

The function of reflective thought, therefore, is to transform a situation in which there is experienced obscurity, doubt, conflict, disturbance of some sort, into a situation that is clear, coherent, settled, harmonious.

—John Dewey, 1933

Of the existing constructs that are commonly used interchangeably when referring to self-supervision (e.g., self-monitoring, self-assessment, self-evaluation, self-reporting, self-management), reflectivity has received the most attention (e.g., Neufeldt, Iverson, & Juntunen, 1995; Neufeldt, Karno, & Nelson, 1996) and has been traced back to Dewey (1933). As described, reflectivity seems to get at the heart of the matter and to encapsulate what self-supervision ultimately strives to accomplish. More specifically, reflectivity has been delineated as a process that involves bracketing personal values, beliefs, and assumptions while looking inwards at internal processes during and after interactions.

☐ The Evolution of Reflectivity

The importance of reflectivity, as it pertains to professional development, has mainly been associated with education (e.g., Copeland, Birmingham, De La Cruz, & Lewin, 1993; McNamara, 1990; Munby & Russell, 1989; Ross; 1989; Roth, 1989; van Merrienboer, Jelsma, & Pass, 1992) and nursing (e.g., Arthur, 1995; G. Mitchell, 1995). More recently, the use of reflectivity to enhance counselor development has been introduced (e.g., Holloway, 1995; Hoshmand, 1994; Hoshmand & Polkinghorne, 1992; Irving & Williams, 1995; Nelson & Neufeldt, 1998; Ward & House, 1998). In essence, reflectivity is considered a valuable exercise whereby counselors can develop their clinical wisdom and professional judgment. Shapiro and Reiff (1993) remarked:

> It is assumed that reflective inquiry by the professional practitioner and cohorts will raise the level of consciousness of the various features of one's practice. This increased awareness, in the author's experience, often results in spotting some inconsistencies or identifying the guiding principles of one's arrangements and uses of personal resources and the constraints which formerly had not been entirely conscious. (p. 1385)

Despite being touted as a principle tool in professional development (Boyd & Fales, 1983), however, Neufeldt et al. (1996) asserted that reflectivity remains somewhat enigmatic. Unfortunately, much the same can be said about the related constructs mentioned at the beginning of this chapter. In other words, although various terms have been used to invite the thoughtful reflection of counselors, there remains scant research data and information pertaining to the precise operationalization and assessment of this process. This point was echoed by Ixer (1999), who was skeptical about the practicality of reflective practice and noted that the extant literature is confusing and contradictory. Although conceding to the proliferation of educational literature on the nature of reflection, he argued that the theorizing about reflectivity "has raised more questions than it has answered and that, in fact, rather little is known, even now, about reflection" (p. 514). Ixer contended that reflective practice as a learning outcome in social work programs should be abandoned. He believed that counselors were vulnerable since mentors commissioned to assess their ability to reflect may have poorly formed conceptions of reflection or conceptions that do not match the counselors'.

In his treatise, Ixer (1999) suggested that social workers needed to respond to rapidly changing situations and could not afford to sit back and reflect on action. In his opinion,

> The pressures engendered, for example, by daily conflicts between resource restrictions, public demands for protection, and the impetus to offer users greater independence present social workers with complex and morally contentious challenges. These require internal processing (cognition), so that external processing in the form of judgement, followed by decision-making (action), can be combined in a speedy response. (p. 519)

Ixer (1999) underscored the differences between professions and the element of time. For example, he discussed how engineers and architects are less often called on to take immediate action, while social workers encounter fast changing and highly challenging information and situations. The point made by Ixer is that in reality not all professionals share the same job pressures or time to reflect on their options.

At the root of Ixer's argument is the valuable question: How does one learn to reflect? This query corresponds with earlier questions by Copeland et al. (1993), such as, What is reflection in practice? How would you recognize a reflective practitioner if you saw one?

Unless a suggested model is carefully scrutinized, potentially useful practices can be perceived as unsubstantial and eventually discarded. Copeland et al. (1993) wrote, "Yet, as has often occurred with other *movements* [italics in original] in education, we are now in danger of being drawn beyond our knowledge base to the employment of practices that are founded in assumptions, rhetoric, and belief in what *should be* [italics in original]" (p. 347). Although new methods to improve the counseling process are enticing, a major concern with moving forward without careful consideration and a healthy dose of skepticism is that the potential lasting benefit of a practice can be wasted if the practice is not monitored and revised appropriately. Rather than abandoning reflective practice due to an absence of rigorous scrutiny and scientific verification, however, a more moderate position is advocated here to augment the self-supervision process. This position encourages professionals to ponder the potential benefits and personal value of this practice. In the end, each professional will determine for himself or herself whether reflection is a useful exercise.

☐ Counselor Self-Awareness and Understanding

Yager and Park (1986) asserted that self-awareness is probably the major obstacle to effective self-supervision and that it is incumbent upon counselors to perform a self-assessment. To assess themselves, however, counselors would need to reflect on their responsibilities and functioning.

Several authors (e.g., Imel, 1992; Ward & House, 1998) have commented that reflecting individuals assume the metaperspective of external observers, work toward identifying assumptions and feelings that underlie their practice, and then speculate about how these assumptions and feelings effect their practice. Bradley (1989) asserted that counselors who are self-aware have matured intellectually, demonstrate complex thinking skills, and can perceive situations from different angles. In summary, she believed that self-aware counselors were highly conscientious, dependable, and able to:

1. understand situations from different perspectives,
2. consider several approaches or solutions to a particular problem,

3. more accurately assess the consequences of the choices they make in given situations, and

4. more effectively evaluate the outcome of their actions.

The ultimate goal of reflection is to explore experiences, create and clarify meaning from these experiences, and increase self-awareness. Although this sounds reasonable in theory, Irving and Williams (1995) contended that reflection is a complex task because it is almost impossible to judge and evaluate personal assumptions from within a personal knowledge framework. These authors explained that assumptions are held to be consistent with the totality of a person's feelings and take on the status of self-evident truths. As a result, assumptions are difficult to identify and question. They also noted that personal experiences are filtered through assumptions and through the unexamined and unconscious theories by which people structure their world, make sense of it, and give meaning to it.

It is probably universally accepted that client self-awareness is a fundamental goal in counseling. Cocreating a safe context wherein clients can become introspective and explore their issues would be a basic goal. As clients are invited to reflect and learn about themselves, professionals can benefit from a similar experience. Lammert (1986) asserted:

> Most therapists agree that the personal issues and perspectives one brings to the helping relationship affect the relationship and, in turn, the client. Although the assumption that it is important and necessary to be aware of self is seldom questioned, this task is a difficult and complex one. (p. 369)

To increase self-awareness, Hackney and Cormier (1996) suggested specific areas that professionals could examine, as detailed in Table 4.1.

TABLE 4.1. Potential Self-Awareness Issues for Enhancing Counselor Reflection

---

1. Awareness of your needs (for example, the need to give or to nurture, the need to be critical, the need to be loved, the need to be respected, the need to be liked, the need to please others, the need to receive approval of others, the need to be right, the need for control).
2. Awareness of your motivation for helping (for example, What do you get or take from helping others? How does helping make you feel good?)
3. Awareness of your feelings (for example, happiness, satisfaction, hurt, anger, sadness, disappointment, confusion, fear).
4. Awareness of your personal strengths, limitations, and coping skills (for example, things about yourself you do well or like, things about yourself you need to work on, how you handle difficulties and stress).

Taken from Hackney and Cormier (1996). Reprinted with permission of Allyn and Bacon, Boston, MA.

In contrasting awareness and insight, Lammert (1986) suggested that the former is a continuing process, "which is readily available over time rather than as special illuminating moments" (p. 374). She also believed that awareness included thinking and feeling and was based on immediate perceptions of current situations. The saliency of this notion has to do with the sense of vigilance inherent in awareness. For example, counselors who value professional awareness work toward remaining sensitive to nuances in counseling rather than waiting for *illuminating moments* to prompt their reflection. Hackney and Cormier (1996) commented that self-awareness and understanding are important because they can help counselors see more objectively and avoid blind spots in their work. It was further proposed that self-awareness and understanding could contribute to greater security and safety for clients and counselors.

Blind spots occur when counselors are unable to understand some aspect of themselves in relation to others. For instance, counselors may criticize clients who do not follow through on assigned homework tasks or relapse and return to problematic behaviors that were apparently under control. When counselors learn about these perceived setbacks, they may demonstrate their concern inappropriately, through verbal (e.g., sarcastic tone) and/or nonverbal (e.g., rolling their eyes, shaking their head in disbelief) behavior.

Rather than reflecting on their feelings of disappointment, anger, or frustration, however, these counselors may consider their reactions to be normal and simply continue the interview, harboring ill feelings toward their clients. It is highly unlikely that counselors who are angry or disappointed with clients are able to suspend this feeling and proceed with the interview in a productive manner. In these situations, counselor emotions generally seep in, influence the tone of an interview, and certainly affect how they respond to clients. Moreover, counselors who are displeased with their clients may begin to see them as resistant, ungrateful, or as obstacles to their own professional success and accomplishment. To protect clients and to ensure that they are provided quality care, counselors are encouraged to work toward self-awareness and understanding. As discussed in Chapter 2, this scenario and the implications associated with unattended counselor distress merits attention.

The correlation that Hackney and Cormier (1996) have drawn between counselor self-awareness and client safety is significant. Counselors who are vigilant about their own moment-to-moment experiences are better prepared and equipped to attend to personal feelings and issues that can influence treatment. As they turn back in on themselves, counselors assume responsibility for their feelings, behavior, and treatment. The following reminders are indeed fundamental but underpin the counseling process.

Remain Client Focused

Helping professionals must be mindful that the counseling context is designed to afford clients opportunities to enter into a process of self-discovery. It is inevitable that this journey will involve unpredictable twists and turns. Rarely is growth a straightforward process. Hence, perceived client setbacks should not be looked upon as an inconvenience or a reflection of counselor competence. The current movement toward brief therapy and rapid elimination of client problems, for example, can place undue pressure on counselors to feel that they are responsible for solving client problems in record time. The sense of urgency created by this thinking can strain and, perhaps, jeopardize the counselor-client relationship when problems persist. Succumbing to this line of thinking can also fuel counselor self-doubt and insecurity. Knowing that counseling seldom provides quick solutions can assist helping professionals to anticipate and accept bumps along the way. Avoiding the urge to work toward rapid problem resolution allows counselors the opportunity to relax, engage clients effectively, and work toward reasonable expectations.

Counseling Is Not a Performance

Clients should not be expected to perform in ways that bolster a counselor's image or self-esteem. Satir (1987) wrote, "When the patient is somehow thought of as a trophy on the therapist's success ladder, this is another repetition of the way in which many children experience their parents—where they were expected to be a show case for family values" (p. 22). In academic or training programs, counselors frequently choose to present audio- or videotapes that illustrate their effectiveness for egocentric reasons. As kudos flow in from colleagues, counselors feel respected, valued, and insightful. Although collegial encouragement and a sense of accomplishment are important, there is an obvious problem with basing one's self-worth and clinical ability on the performance of clients. That is, counselors may unknowingly pressure clients to follow suggested interventions in search of the ultimate solution. Feeling that their reputations are on the line, counselors may become aggressive and demanding. As noted by Kottler and Hazler (1997), a counselor may respond to the sense of urgency expressed by the significant others of a client, worry about how these people will evaluate his or her clinical competency, and thus feel pressured to solve the presenting problem.

When counselors become overzealous, clients may also be hesitant to accurately report their progress for fear of disappointing the counselor. In one clinical situation, for example, a client was reluctant to inform his counselor that he decided on an alternative plan of action because he did not want to disappoint the professional helper. Another client was providing inaccurate reports about her weight because she believed that the truth about her weight loss would upset her counselor. Cerney (1995) addressed how clients may sacrifice personal needs for the well-being and comfort of therapists. She wrote, "At the slightest hint of displeasure or disbelief on the part of the therapist, the patient will avoid that particular painful topic and go on to a more acceptable subject" (p. 133).

Embedded in these stories are both positive and negative elements. On the one hand, it appears that the clients in these scenarios felt committed toward their counselors. It could be assumed that the counselors described in these former scenarios were effective in forming a close working relationship with their clients. On the other hand, on some level, the helping professional may have inadvertently transgressed a boundary and perhaps became overinvolved in the counseling relationship. As previously noted, there are far-reaching ramifications associated with becoming overinvolved and losing objectivity.

There is always a third hypothesis: that clients are afraid to accurately report their status. To avoid being criticized for their perceived lack of commitment, clients may misinform their counselors. Feeling re-wounded by counselors can distort clients' perception of the helping relationship, perpetuate their victimization, and/or contribute to their premature withdrawal from treatment. Rather than perceiving the counseling context as safe, clients can feel threatened and vulnerable. This scenario was witnessed within an adolescent inpatient treatment setting where a young client felt controlled and intimidated by her counselor. Knowing that the counselor could influence her approaching discharge date, she disguised her true moods, remained very compliant, and praised the counselor for his work. Although successful in being discharged, the youngster was eventually readmitted under the charge of another clinician.

Grosch and Olsen (1994) proposed that unrealistic counselor expectations may be manifested in terms of expectations of client growth. In other words, the same drive that propels counselors to help and to be seen as helpful often cultivates unrealistic ideas about client change. Grosch and Olsen wrote:

> Great expectations on the part of the therapist with regard to client growth not only interfere with the process of psychotherapy but may also lead to burnout. If the therapist needs clients to change, he or she is in trouble. On the one hand, the client will most likely feel the pressure of the therapist to get well, as a way of making the therapist feel better. On the other hand, if the client does not get better, the therapist may feel ineffective and frustrated. (p. 16)

☐ Counselor Motivation versus Counselor Coercion

It is important to draw a distinction between motivating strategies and pressuring tactics that are employed by counselors. The former involves encouraging clients to work toward problem resolution at their own pace. Motivating counselors are likened to inspiring coaches who keep their clients' best interests in mind. They understand that clients are the best judges of what they can or cannot do and thus avoid pushing clients toward uncharted territory. They continually reflect on their own motives and do not base their clinical competence on client progress.

Counselors who place unrealistic demands on themselves tend to employ coercive behaviors and are critical of clients who show minimal or no progress. Clearly, for these professionals, their clinical worth hinges on client progress. Needless to say, the emotional burden they impose upon themselves is unnecessary and counterproductive. Satir (1987) remarked that, "There are those therapists who feel challenged to make something of the patient, *even if it kills you* [italics in original]" (p. 22).

Case Vignette

Gail was a community-based psychiatric nurse who worked with clients presenting with a myriad of emotional and behavioral problems. In her practice, she witnessed a range of clients who, for the most part, reported rapid stabilization. One case that particularly concerned Gail involved a young man who continually complained about "his life going nowhere." Despite Gail's efforts to problem-solve with and motivate her client, there was little evidence of progress. Gail's client remained unemployed and reliant on community services and a monthly welfare check.

Over time, Gail began to feel that she was failing her client and began to question her clinical competence. After several sessions, Gail disclosed to her client that she was considering referring him to a colleague. When discussing her rationale, she explained that she felt that she had exhausted all of her ideas and that both she and the client were stuck. After carefully listening, the client asked why Gail was in such a hurry for things to change. Although it was a seemingly innocent question, Gail found herself questioning her own motives. After agreeing that she would reconsider her plan, Gail returned to her office and began to reflect on the importance that she was placing on rapid client improvement. After some thought, she discovered that a large majority of her clients demonstrated a degree of stabilization and improvement after several sessions. However, it became very clear to her that clients who returned with persistent problems caused her grief. More importantly, Gail began to question whether her decision to refer clients was simply a convenient way to avoid a level of personal discomfort and embarrassment during monthly case reviews that involved other team members. Gail was beginning to make the connection between client improvement and her concern for her clinical reputation and status.

In addition to jeopardizing the counseling relationship, counselors who overextend themselves as a result of idealism and lofty expectations are at risk of burnout. Such counselors assume too much responsibility and feel tremendous pressure to succeed.

☐ Reflecting for Personal Growth

As noted by Stickel and Trimmel (1994), "Reflection is an emergent process that goes beyond defining oneself as Rogerian, or an eclectic counselor, or a user of reality therapy" (p. 108). Stickel and Trimmel addressed the process of developing one's own voice during the reflection process. They noted that, "The taking of an *I* [italics in original] voice is one of the goals of the reflective process and is critical for meeting new professional challenges" (p. 104). In describing the reflective process this way, these authors accentuated the issue of personal accountability. Within this process, professionals confront themselves by questioning their motives and actions in search of enhanced self-awareness. With increased self-awareness, professionals become more sensitive to the environment and entertain new conceptual perspectives. As a result of their pause and deliberation, professionals may benefit from restructuring their perception of a troubling situation, the emergence of new knowledge, and multiple explanations. Without having the pressure to solve presenting problems, counselors are afforded opportunities to engage in internal dialogue. According to Ward and House (1998), a secondary characteristic of reflective dialogue is an emphasis on self-assessment. They reported that this internal process is characterized by an ability to "reflect objectively on the counseling process in relation to the needs of clients" (p. 29) and suggested that the following questions promote self-assessment: What hypotheses are possible for explaining the client's or family's needs? Do you have the skills to address these needs effectively and ethically? If not, what do you have to do to address this gap?

Ward and House (1998) broach the critical issue of ethics. With careful reflection, counselors can honestly ask themselves whether they are equipped to provide service to specific clinical populations. This issue has proven to be highly contentious among counselors, particularly those who work in isolated or rural areas. These professionals report that they do not have the luxury of selecting clients who would be suitable based on their expertise. Since they usually work in isolation, these counselors are expected to deal with a wide range of problems despite their lack of training. Unfortunately, in these situations, both counselors and clients are at risk ethically and professionally. Imagine, for example, untrained counselors who are asked to deal with cases of domestic violence, child abuse, or suicidal behaviors. In the end, it will be counselors who will assess their own ability to help specific clients. The reflective process might help counselors in discerning if they possess the skills to proceed effectively and ethically.

Reflection concerns how professionals conceptualize puzzling or perplexing situations. Neufeldt (1997) remarked that counselors should be encouraged to develop hypotheses based on interactions with clients as well as prior knowledge and clinical experience. She also noted that hypotheses should be tested with moment-by-moment interventions in sessions and that client responses to interventions need to be examined in light of the counselor's hypotheses. Reflectivity, therefore, is a means for reliving and recapturing experience to understand it, learn from it, and develop new insights and appreciations. Through the reflective process, the less obvious aspects of one's experience become more apparent and can be connected to present and future activities.

Reflection-in-Action

Although the term *reflect* tends to connote a return to past events, Schon (1983) contends that practitioners frequently think about what they are doing while doing it. Therefore, the immediacy of reflection should not be overlooked. Schon recognized that reflection-in-action was a contradiction in terms and addressed the concern about reflection-in-action interfering with and paralyzing one's ability to act spontaneously. As Schon (1983) pointed out, reflection is not relegated to a period of time following a meaningful event but can occur spontaneously during the event. He further contended that learning cannot take place without reflection wherein practitioners make sense of or extract meaning from their experiences. It is not unusual, for example, to watch reflecting counselors become contemplative following a client statement. It is as if client information goes through a filter before a response is rendered. Slowly, counselors consider statements and their interpretations. Such counselors often request time within the interview room to reflect or arrange for a short break. By following their own pace, they avoid being controlled and interrupted by internal pressure (e.g., anxiety) or external pressure (e.g., community demands). During a recent class devoted to counselor self-care, a student questioned whether it was appropriate for professionals to spontaneously interrupt a counseling session in order to secure private time to reflect on consequential client information before responding. The student believed that such behavior might strain the counselor-client relationship and interfere with the counseling process. It was suggested that, depending on the context and information, it could indeed be appropriate for counselors to request a brief interlude to thoughtfully consider potential responses.

This debate is particularly important in light of Eraut's (1995) challenge to Schon's (1983) notion of reflection-in-action. Eraut argued that as soon as counselors turn in on themselves, they have cognitively, if not physically, left the action. From his perspective, counselors who reflect-in-action interrupt the action, rather than reflect on it. Hence, the question of whether counselors can effectively attend to clients while they are in the process of reflection arises. To assert that all counselors are incapable of reflection while they are in process with clients would be an erroneous generalization. Questions about how and when counselors reflect during their interactions with clients become important. Finally, whether it is possible for counselors *not to* reflect enters the debate.

During the aforementioned student discussion it was emphasized that there are times when a physical interlude is not possible due to the gravity of a situation. An example was presented to the student that involved an adolescent boy at a residential treatment center. When this youngster's immediate demand to meet with the executive director was denied, he went outside, pulled a hedge from its roots, and tossed the hedge through a large clinic window. Not only was the youngster successful in startling the clerical staff, but he escalated the situation by selecting a piece of the shattered glass, placing it against his raised arm, and screaming, "Is this what it takes to get your attention?" After hearing the commotion in the reception area, the executive director, who was also a clinical psychologist, began to attend to the youngster and successfully de-escalated the crisis.

The point here is that, due to the critical nature of the situation, the executive director did not have the opportunity to request a brief recess in order to reflect on the situation and his options. Instead, he immediately responded to the critical incident. Such an example exemplifies Schon's (1983) notion that professionals can think as they act. While some professionals schedule times during their sessions to reflect or consult, others prefer to take this time only as necessary. Regardless of preference, it is important for counselors to take time to reflect as needed.

Further, reflection should not be associated with professionals quietly resting as they contemplate their options. Obviously, as illustrated in the preceding case vignette, this is not always possible. In reality, counselors encounter formidable clinical challenges that require them to think on their feet.

The example described above addresses a concern that has been raised by Ixer (1999) regarding the usefulness of reflective practice with intense clinical situations. He wrote,

In social work, the practitioner is faced with changing and highly challenging problematic information, and is required to exercise judgement under extreme pressure, knowing that the consequence of not *getting it right* [italics in original] can be a child abuse enquiry or a judicial review. (p. 517)

Ixer's concern is well taken and underlines the complexity of human service work. The following case vignette further exemplifies how counselors are expected to rapidly reflect on critical situations and intervene appropriately.

Case Vignette

A child welfare worker and a family therapist were making a planned home visit with a high-risk family to assess the family environment. As they entered the doorway, the professionals had to sidestep piles of soiled clothing and contend with a foul odor. To their dismay, empty beer bottles were scattered throughout the living room and a visitor was semiconscious in a chair. Two boys ran freely in and out of the house, ignoring their mother's command to slow down. The mother appeared disheveled and began to behave obnoxiously when queried about the well-being of her children. Despite attempts from both professionals to calm the mother, she became increasingly irritable and verbally aggressive toward the child welfare worker. Realizing that the situation was escalating, and concerned about the welfare of the children, the child welfare worker pulled his colleague aside and asked about an immediate apprehension of the children. Before offering his opinion, the family therapist had to quickly reflect on a number of salient factors, including (a) the steps required to carry out an apprehension order, (b) the legal ramifications associated with carrying out an apprehension order, (c) the psychological implications associated with separating the boys from their mother, (d) the potential impact of substitute care on the boys, and (e) the future relationship between the mother and the helping professionals.

Focusing on the Positive

When addressing fundamental questions regarding reflectivity, Copeland et al. (1993) underscored important issues that directly relate to self-supervision. First, they pointed out how the term *problem solving* carries a pejorative connotation and suggests arriving at a single correct solution. As discussed in Chapter 5, an emphasis on counselor strengths and curiosity is recommended for the self-supervision process. When adhering to a problem-focused framework, counselors are apt to overlook their strengths and potential and eventually search for deficits. Of course, there will be points during treatment when counselors wish they could have responded differently. However, these instances are usually greatly outnumbered by times when they responded effectively.

Second, the idea of having to solve a problem places unnecessary pressure on counselors. In search of solutions, counselors may risk inadvertently jeopardizing relationships with clients. As their minds are working fervently on designing strategies, counselors become distracted by multiple tasks, fail to carefully listen to client narratives, and do not notice client nuances. It becomes a needless race against time.

In general, the problem-solving approach also conflicts with reflective practice in that the recursive process of counselor modification is ignored. Professionals who are committed to self-supervision work toward remaining in tune with client feedback in order to adjust their responses. Reflective counselors consider past experiences and present situations and enter into meaningful thought about their philosophical beliefs. Reflective practice permeates the work of counselors and is interwoven in the fabric of the counseling process. It is worth reiterating that counselor reflection is not a technique but rather an underlying philosophy that can guide a counselor's practice throughout his or her career (Nelson & Neufledt, 1998).

☐ Necessary Attitudes for Reflective Thinking

It would also be unrealistic to assume that all counselors are interested, psychologically ready, or have the cognitive ability to abstractly think about themselves in relation to others. This comment is not intended to be derogatory of professionals who do not think about their relationships with clients or their interventions. Obviously, professionals have strengths in different areas. Developmentally, some counselors may still need experience to appreciate this arduous process. Such counselors may not have arrived at a point in their career where they have come to understand the intricacies inherent in human interactions, particularly in treatment. Over time, they may begin to realize the complex nature of their work and the benefit of reflecting on their belief systems, assumptions, and internal/external responses.

It should also be underlined that an inability to reflect on relationships does not immediately translate into professional incompetence or a disinterest in client welfare. Some professionals appear to possess an aptitude to unravel connections that exist between their behaviors and client responses on a cognitive level. When acknowledging the systemic basis of human relationships, counselors consider their part during clinical interactions.

☐ Removing Roadblocks to Reflectivity

According to Dewey (1933), a lack of authentic counselor reflection can be attributed to several factors that are described below and whose antidotes include open-mindedness, wholeheartedness, and intellectual responsibility.

Open-Mindedness

Dewey (1933) referred to open-mindedness as "a freedom from prejudice, partisanship, and such other habits as close the mind and make it unwilling to consider new problems and entertain new ideas" (p. 30). For open-mindedness to emerge, and for counselors to avoid the trap of certainty, the elements of curiosity and patience are indeed essential ingredients. In addressing the notion of openness, Baker (1996) proposed that professionals required time to absorb information from different sources and to allow for a *percolation* period. As a result, professionals must allay their internal anxieties and forgo quick and perhaps hasty solutions. As described above, even in crisis intervention scenarios, time (although collapsed) and patience are necessary. The popular television series *ER* attempts to depict this concept very well despite its frequent overdramatization. Although facing potentially fatal situations, the emergency room physicians request and absorb critical information prior to embarking on a major intervention. In spite of cries from less experienced colleagues to rush into what appear to be needed interventions, the more experienced physicians mentally work through patient needs and procedures. This process also exemplifies Schon's (1983) reflection-in-action, wherein each move is predicated on the last.

Although obvious differences exist between critical and noncritical counseling situations, the issue of time and patience must not be overlooked. During crisis intervention, counselors need to avoid panic reactions and the temptation to move hastily. Remaining calm when considering options and client information should not be mistaken as indifference. In fact, professionals who assume a tentative stance may be displaying enormous attention and concern. They take time and postpone decisions in order to consider a situation from different angles. During this period, professionals may be reflecting on their repertoire of life or clinical experiences, client information, and context. This process consolidates and synthesizes information, albeit very rapidly.

Following an interval of openness, Baker (1996) reported that professionals may enter an "aha stage," when they feel that they have experienced change and learned something. This stage is perceived as spontaneous, liberating, and instrumental in launching professionals in a different direction. With new ideas to pursue, professionals realize that they have not necessarily solved the problem but have created new inroads for themselves and their clients. As previously noted, assuming that a *problem* is solved (and thus adhering to a problem-solving approach) sets professionals up to believe that their task is to solve problems rather than search for different meanings and personal modification.

Tradition: Helpful or Restrictive?

The process of reflection challenges established knowledge and tradition. Mitchell (1995), for example, stated that reflection can be perceived as a "pivotal process of breaking with the known and accepted, or in other words, of breaking with tradition" (p. 57). Although appearing straightforward at first glance, the reflective process involves challenging the status quo and strongly held assumptions and values.

When elaborating on the notion of open-mindedness, Dewey (1933) promoted an open stance and the importance of (a) possessing an active desire to listen to more sides than one, (b) giving heed to facts from whatever source they come, (c) giving full attention to alternative possibilities, and (d) recognizing the possibility of error even in strongly held beliefs. He further listed three hindrances to open-mindedness: mental sluggishness, self-conceit, and unconscious fears. Mental sluggishness develops when professionals are adamant about assuming the work associated is challenging their own beliefs. Although remaining closed to new ideas is less threatening, it perpetuates a mental rut. Moving out of a comfort zone in order to entertain new perspectives involves risk and, perhaps, a level of emotional discomfort. During this process, professionals embark on a process that challenges their existing schemata about self, others, and the world in general. Mitchell (1995) elaborated: "It is suggested here that the process of reflection not only discloses inconsistencies and unacceptable beliefs in light of desired ideals; reflection also prompts movement toward the strange and unfamiliar. Engaging what is strange surfaces discomfort and uncertainty" (p. 57). Baker (1996) equated this internal discomfort with the experience of "knowing that there is something that one must do but being unable to remember what it is" (p. 20). When discovering new information about oneself, professionals are faced with the task of having to reconcile their new conceptions with their old beliefs. Imel (1992) further remarked that reflective practice "can also be a tool for revealing discrepancies between espoused theories (what we say we do) and theories-in-use (what we actually do)."

Self-conceit can be defined as a reluctance of professionals to admit that a belief that they have held dearly is wrong. Such professionals have convinced themselves that their position is correct, and any challenge to a strongly held belief system is met with resistance. When looking further into the issue of self-conceit, professional insecurity surfaces. In other words, professionals who struggle with input regarding their ideas or positions may personalize feedback and perceive it as a personal attack. Rather than listening to colleagues or clients, insecure professionals immediately assume a defensive stance.

Unconscious fears can provoke a sense of alarm in professionals who assume a defensive stance to protect a position. Unfortunately, in an effort to defend themselves, professionals become blinded to new observations and conceptions. When unconscious fears prevail, professionals guard against opposing views and enter into a protective mode. Consequently, as professionals enter into a protective mode and withdraw, new learning is unlikely to occur. Although adhering to traditional thought and behavior can provide professionals with a sense of assurance, familiarity, and comfort, there may be costs associated with this decision. From a scientific perspective, for example, Mitchell (1995) questioned who might benefit from unexamined tradition and wondered about the cost associated with this practice. She drew an analogy between tradition and the sacred cow metaphor, providing examples from the nursing profession, and discussed objectivity, the nursing process, nursing diagnosis, verification, replication, control, manipulation, and standardization. From Mitchell's (1995) perspective, tradition can diminish professional responsibility and accountability. A significant question emerging from this argument becomes: Is it the professional helper or the client who is better served by tradition? Clearly not all professionals consider reflection an opportunity to create new ways of knowing and improving practice. For some, it is a very unsettling and potentially destructive process that can lead to personal threat and distress.

Wholeheartedness

The notion of wholeheartedness refers to a process whereby individuals feel a deep passion for a subject and thus put their hearts and souls into it. These individuals are absorbed, and a natural, genuine interest ensues. Dewey (1933) suggested that wholeheartedness is demonstrated by professionals who show a veritable stake in their thought process, which "buoys the mind up and gives an onward impetus to thinking" (p. 32). Dewey also asserted that individuals who are passionate about a subject area are less likely to become distracted or require external motivation. They are essentially fueled by their ebullience.

Intellectual Responsibility

Dewey (1933) wrote the following about intellectual responsibility:

to be intellectually responsible is to consider the consequences of a pro-
jected step; it means to be willing to adopt these consequences when they
follow reasonably from any position already taken. Intellectual responsibility
secures integrity; that is to say, consistence and harmony in belief. (p. 32)

This perspective spawns a sense of professional accountability for one's
cognitive process and ultimate behavior. Professionals who are intellectually responsible go beyond a superficial level and are truly invested in
seeking the meaning behind words and behaviors. The notion of intellectual responsibility further emphasizes the rigorous process involved in
thinking about potential responses and the importance of what is and is
not said between counselors and clients. Based on this perspective, the
opinion that counseling is merely a casual conversation between professionals and client is challenged.

☐ Practical Strategies for Reflective Practice

It is always helpful to have a map before traveling into uncharted territory, and embarking on the reflective process is no exception. Roth (1989)
provided an extensive list and a guideline of sorts summarizing reflective
processes. Essentially, it is a list of do's that counselors can follow for
effective self-reflection, as provided in Table 4.2.

Practicality of Reflection

To provide a balanced view of reflectivity, its practicality and the time
required to reflect must be addressed. Clearly, reflection is time consuming and involves a certain degree of personal risk (Imel, 1992). Shapiro
and Reiff (1993) addressed the practicality of reflection and wrote:

> However, reflection in (during) practice it seems to us, is very difficult to
> accomplish for the busy practitioner, beset by multiple demands and, if
> anything, an overload of professional knowledge. . . . It is our contention,
> then, that satisfactory reflection is a somewhat fragile skill and requires the
> perspective of a meta-position. (p. 1380)

Allocating time to reflect involves a commitment to personal well-being
and professional development. It is unlikely that this practice will be encouraged by all public or private agencies in which emphasis is placed on
the number of clients served as opposed to the quality of service provided. Many professionals who work in community-based agencies can
attest to the funding crunch and the drive toward increased caseloads and
service. Little, if any, time is devoted to professional introspection and
development.

TABLE 4.2. Essential Ingredients for Counselor Reflection

1. Question what, why, and how one does things, and ask what, why, and how others do things.
2. Emphasize inquiry as a tool of learning.
3. Suspend judgment, wait for sufficient data, or self-validate.
4. Seek alternatives.
5. Keep an open mind.
6. Compare and contrast.
7. Seek the framework, theoretical basis, and/or underlying rationale (of behaviors, methods, techniques, programs).
8. View from various perspectives.
9. Identify and test assumptions (theirs and others); seek conflicting evidence.
10. Put into different/varied contexts.
11. Ask "What if . . . ?"
12. Ask for others' ideas and viewpoints.
13. Adapt and adjust to instability and change.
14. Function within uncertainty, complexity, and variety.
15. Hypothesize.
16. Consider consequences.
17. Validate what is given or believed.
18. Synthesize and test.
19. Seek, identify, and resolve problems ("problem setting", "problem solving").
20. Initiate after thinking through (alternatives, consequences) or putting into context.
21. Analyze: What makes it work? In what context would it not?
22. Evaluate: What worked, what didn't, and why?
23. Use prescriptive models (behavioral models, protocols) only when adapted to the situation.
24. Make decisions in practice of the profession (knowledge created in use).

Roth, copyright 1989 in the Journal of Teacher Education. Reprinted with permission of Sage Publications, Inc.

Deciding what issue to pursue can also be overwhelming for counselors. Because of the increased number of clients and the heightened severity of client problems (e.g., Hickson & Baltimore, 1998), counselors can experience a myriad of emotions. For example, during the course of a day, counselors can experience anger, delight, and sadness when working with clients. The challenge lies in identifying a theme or issue that emerges consistently (e.g., worry about client recovery) and connecting it to other life issues (e.g., need to succeed at work).

Counselors working with clients who present with similar presenting problems (e.g., sexual abuse, substance abuse, domestic violence) may be especially prone to mental sluggishness. Because they hear minor variations of the same problems on a regular basis, they report a lack of interest in details since they have heard them all before! One counselor who worked at a women's shelter described how she found herself simply processing clients. She explained that, over time, client stories of abuse all came to sound the same.

Opening oneself up to constructive feedback can be part and parcel of the reflective process. As discussed with the proposed self-supervision model described in Chapter 5, asking clients for feedback may not come easily for all professionals. The information shared by clients may be unexpected and painful. Nevertheless, only by asking for honest feedback can counselors learn about themselves.

Johari's Awareness Model

A very simple and useful instrument that can help professionals obtain information about themselves from others is the Johari window. The Johari window divides the individual into four quandrants, as illustrated in Table 4.3. "Each quadrant represents an area of awareness on the part of the individual and the person with whom he interacts. Awareness refers to knowledge of behavior, feelings, and motivation" (Hansen, Stevic, & Warner, 1977, p. 277).

Although the window is divided into four quadrants, each quadrant is not necessarily the same size. For example, an individual may not be very open about the self, and therefore, quadrant 1 would be larger in comparison to the other quadrants. In reference to self-reflection, it could be hypothesized that professionals considered suitable for quadrant 1 would have a good understanding of themselves and be open to feedback. Hansen, Stevic, and Warner (1977) asserted that, "The larger the open quadrant, the greater the individual's contact with reality and the more available his abilities and needs are to himself and those around him" (p. 277).

TABLE 4.3. Johari Window Quadrants

Quandrant 1: OPEN	**Quadrant 2: BLIND**
The open quadrant consists of material about self that is known to both the individual and the person with whom he or she interacts.	The blind quadrant consists of material about the self that is known by others but is not recognized by the individual.
Quadrant 3: HIDDEN	**Quadrant 4: UNKNOWN**
The hidden quadrant consists of that material about the self of which the individual is aware but which is not known to people with whom he or she interacts.	The unknown quadrant consists of material about the self that is out of awareness of both the individual and the other person.

Taken from Hansen, Stevic, and Warner (1977). Reprinted with permission of Allyn and Bacon, Boston, MA.

Following this model, it stands to reason that professionals who are rigid, insecure, and protective about their views would probably fall into quadrants 2, 3, and 4. To move oneself out of quadrants 2, 3, or 4, interpersonal learning on behalf of professionals would have to occur. Again, such progression can be understood within a developmental framework. In other words, patience and time is required for professionals to become less anxious about leaving their comfort zones.

The Johari window provides counselors with a framework from within which to explore themselves. For example, a counselor can ask a trusted colleague to comment on his or her behaviors with clients. From this exchange, the counselor might discover information that was previously out of his or her awareness. One counselor, for example, learned that he frequently enjoyed his favorite beverage while interviewing clients. Although he considered this habit to be innocent enough, it was pointed out to him that he never extended the same offer to his clients. It was further pointed out to the counselor that such behavior could be perceived as impolite and rude by some clients.

☐ Reflectivity: A Developmental Framework

Ross (1989) summarized work completed by Kitchner and King and presented a very useful chart that outlined stages in the development of reflective judgement. This chart is reviewed below and can help professionals to understand how the process of reflection evolves and becomes increasingly complex over time.

Early Stage

Individuals in the early stages of developing reflective judgment generally see the world in a simplistic, black-and-white manner. To them, there are absolutes, and those in positions of authority are privileged holders of knowledge. These characteristics are not uncommon among beginning counselors, who tend to regard supervisors or popular theorists as gurus. Instead of questioning the position of their luminaries and asking for evidence to support their grandiose claims, individuals desperate for *answers* and *formulas* myopically follow direction based on good faith.

The field of counseling is replete with quick fixes endorsed by charismatic, articulate, and convincing individuals who assert, "Trust me, it works." A drawback to this trend was noted by Gibbs and Gambrill (1999), who wrote, "Slick emotional appeals can block critical thinking about any subject" (p. 41). When moving beyond superficial assurances and marketing ploys, however, counselors soon discover that minimal or no research has been conducted to support inflated claims. Miller, Duncan, and Hubble (1997) provided a sobering review of psychotherapy outcomes and reported that no one theory, model, or combination of techniques is better than any other. They wrote, "While the proponents of a particular model may cite the occasional study demonstrating the superiority of their particular approach, the preponderance of the data indicates that no meaningful difference exists" (p. 2). Unfortunately, honest and accurate appraisals of various counseling theories and techniques are few. It appears that professionals latch onto theoretical frameworks and strategies that are personally appealing but not necessarily suitable for clients. Irving and Williams (1995) elaborated in the following extract:

> For example, one counsellor might hold the assumption that the foundation of such a relationship is *support* [italics in original], which entails emphasis on the positive, minimization of the negative, and protection of the client. Another counsellor might hold the assumption that the foundation of the relationship is *authority* [italics in original], which entails telling clients what their thoughts, feelings and actions mean and telling them what they should do to cope better with their lives. And, of course, the client may hold assumptions about the nature of the *required* [italics in original] relationship which differs from those of the counsellor. (p. 109)

Middle Stages

During the middle stages, individuals begin to demonstrate a healthy cynicism and acknowledge different perspectives. No longer wedded to a single view, these individuals begin to flex their mental muscles and question the validity of claims. Their former certainty about issues loosens, and room is created for additional thought. Despite their growth, however, individuals in the middle stages tend to revert to unsupported personal beliefs when making decisions. Although their critical reflective process has matured, old habits persist and require ongoing attention. This tendency is often prevalent in crisis situations. In an attempt to relieve personal anxiety, professionals retreat to their previous comfort zone. This process is very evident in training centers where professionals are invited to conceptualize presenting problems differently and intervene in ways in which they are unaccustomed. During role-plays, such professionals are generally able to successfully translate a new theory into practice. They begin to struggle, however, when they attempt to do so with actual clients. During moments of doubt, they return to previous thinking and clinical behavior.

Later Stages

The later stages are marked by an appreciation for multiple perspectives and integration of ideas. During this period, professionals are less likely to embrace definitive positions and more likely to appreciate diversity. To assume this particular stance, professionals need to reach a stage wherein they are comfortable with uncertainty. From a developmental perspective, it would be unreasonable to presume that novice professionals could immediately become reflective about their work. Many beginning professionals have to deal with a myriad of demands associated with their new jobs. Consequently, time and experience will play a vital role in the development of reflective skills.

Stages in the Development of Reflective Judgment

Stages 1 and 2
- Views world as simple
- Believes knowledge to be absolute
- Views authorities as the source of all knowledge

Stage 3
- Acknowledges existence of differences of viewpoints
- Believes knowledge to be relative
- Sees varying positions about issues as equally right or equally wrong
- Uses unsupported personal belief as frequently as "hard" evidence in making decisions
- Views truth as "knowable" but not yet known

Stage 4
- Perceives legitimate differences of viewpoint
- Develops a beginning ability to interpret evidence
- Uses unsupported personal belief and evidence in making decisions, but is beginning to be able to differentiate between them
- Believes that knowledge is uncertain in some areas

Stages 5 and 6
- Views knowledge as contextually based
- Develops views that an integrated perspective can be evaluated as more or less likely to be true
- Develops initial ability to integrate evidence into a coherent point of view

Stage 7
- Exhibits all characteristics listed in Stages 5 and 6
- Possesses ability to make objective judgments based on reasoning and evidence
- Is able to modify judgments based on new evidence if necessary

☐ Coloring Outside the Lines

Brookfield (1987) believed that critical thinking was a lived activity—not an abstract academic pasttime—that could be observed in the contexts of our personal relationships, work activities, and political endeavors. He further stated that critical thinking "involves calling into question the assumptions underlying our customary, habitual ways of thinking and acting and then being ready to think and act differently on the basis of this critical questioning" (p. 2). What can be extracted from this statement is the courage, integrity, and risk inherent in critical thinking. Helping professionals who challenge established clinical procedures, techniques, or models are vulnerable to being criticized and ostracized. Such professionals constantly wonder and are not afraid to ask questions. According to Gibbs and Gambrill (1999), "Critical thinkers make a genuine effort to critique fairly all views, preferred and unpreferred. They value accuracy over *winning* [italics in original] or social approval" (p. 4).

Arnold and Boggs (1995) contended that, "Critical thinking is based on the premise that it is as important to learn *how* [italics in original] to learn as it is to learn about specific content" (p. 377). All too often professionals gravitate and subscribe to a popular idea without carefully examining its merit. These authors went on to state that when faced with the unknown, some people tend to accept a simplistic explanation of a problem definition and treatment plan. Others simply give up in frustration because they do not believe that there is a reasonable explanation, and resort to conventional methods. For example, it is not unusual for clinicians, when faced with what appear to be bizarre behaviors, to immediately categorize clients according to the DSM-IV (American Psychiatric Association, 1994). In addition, the thought of prescribing medication becomes the instantaneous and only form of treatment. In reality, these clinicians are unsure what to attribute the behavior to and find solace in traditional categorization and intervention.

For some counselors, challenging the status quo might call into question their competency. In other words, the counselor's perception might be challenged. Although such professionals firmly believe in what they think, they fear an onslaught of objections and reprisals.

The perceived inability or reluctance of helping professionals to think critically about clients or situations can be attributed to a variety of reasons. Keeley, Shemberg, Cowell, and Zinnbauer (1995), for instance, discussed student fear and elaborated on different ways to ameliorate this feeling. Obviously not everyone is comfortable in stating an alternative (and sometimes radical) position. Depending on the context, helping professionals may be fearful of criticism. As outlined below, Brookfield (1987) described several valuable propositions regarding critical thinking.

Critical Thinking Is a Productive and Positive Activity

Critical thinkers are vibrant and innovative individuals who are invested in re-creating ways to improve client welfare. Such professionals are receptive to new ideas that are geared toward positive change. Regardless of how foreign an idea may sound, critical thinkers approach each idea respectfully and with an open mind to ensure that opposing points of view are presented. Unfortunately, those who show interest by asking important (and sometimes awkward) questions are often perceived as cynical, disrespectful, and ignorant. In fact, their curiosity is considered oppositional and disruptive to the regular process. Several authors (e.g., Goodman, 1984; Schmidt & Davidson, 1983) referred to this questioning behavior as supportive dissent and challenge. Such reframing begins to illustrate that critical thinkers are invested in assuming a multiperspectival position from which to consider alternative views.

Examples of how critical thinking is discouraged or dismissed are plentiful in counseling case conferences. For example, when professionals challenge a treatment protocol and suggest different ways of helping clients, their efforts are politely dismissed and regarded as provocative or inappropriate. Such reactions even occur when existing treatment plans are failing miserably. However, rather than changing course and entertaining new ideas, those responsible for treatment continue with the same line of action. In doing so, such professionals tend to associate a lack of clinical progress with client resistance or a lack of time. Rather than restructure the problem and rethink their treatment plan, professionals continue to use the same strategies without success, thus repeating a problematic pattern (Watzlawick, Weakland, & Fisch, 1974). Critical thinking is not about who is right or wrong. As Brookfield (1987) so aptly stated, by thinking critically, "we gain an awareness that others in the world have the same sense of certainty we do—but about ideas, values, and actions that are completely contrary to our own" (p. 5). In assuming a nonadversarial stance, professionals begin to encourage colleagues to passionately express ideas, particularly ideas that are contrary to their own. Within this context, oppression is avoided and diversity is celebrated.

Critical Thinking Is a Process, Not an Outcome

An attractive aspect of critical thinking is the element of continuation. The process of critical thinking entails a continual questioning of assumptions and beliefs. It would be erroneous to consider critical thinking as having an end point where awareness has been fully realized. Doing so would go against a basic tenet of critical thinking, which discourages any claim to universal truth or total certainty (Brookfield, 1987).

Helping professionals who are dissatisfied with superficial answers and who seek deeper meaning face a balancing act when interacting with colleagues and clients. For some, the persistent inquisitiveness of reflective skeptics can be interpreted as bothersome, suspicious, and time consuming. Nevertheless, critical thinkers pay attention to the process of reasoning, not just to the product (Gibbs & Gambrill, 1999).

Manifestations of Critical Thinking Vary According to Context

Critical thinking can be demonstrated in a variety of ways and is not isolated to the spoken or written word. Depending on personal preferences, professionals can indicate that they have weighed a suggestion or recommendation. Although some professionals may verbalize how they have arrived at a decision, others may do so nonverbally. For example, counselors who are encouraged to consider the importance of allowing clients to finish their statements before speaking may show that they have understood the reasoning of this recommendation through their behavior with clients. One counselor, for example, sat on his hands after speaking. Only after the client finished did he remove his hands and respond.

Critical Thinking Is Triggered by Both Positive and Negative Events

As noted in the previous chapter, critical thinking does not always follow a negative event. Although it is conceded that counselors who assume a problem-solving approach to treatment generally reflect on the negative aspects of one's clinical work, positive events can also prompt critical thinking. For example, professionals who discover that they are capable of effectively engaging supposedly *resistant* clients have the opportunity to think about how they did so. Rather than chalking it up to luck, these professionals can carefully reflect on their decision-making process and interpersonal skills throughout an interview. During these times, professionals are afforded opportunities to reinterpret past actions and ideas from a new vantage point (Brookfield, 1987).

Critical Thinking is Both Emotive and Rational

As reiterated throughout this book, the process of reflecting and thinking critically about self, others, and human service is laden with emotion. Anxiety, fear, resentment, joy, and ambivalence can result when professionals decide to pursue deeper meaning and different ways of looking at the world. Clearly, there is cognitive activity involved when thinking deeply about an issue or situation but this endeavor also involves emotion. Professionals who question the beliefs, values, and assumptions underlying their own practice enter into uncharted waters not knowing what awaits them.

Paul (1990) helped to clarify the process of critical thinking by drawing an important distinction between critical thinking and what he refers to as uncritical thinking. Each concept is outlined in Table 4.4.

In relation to counselor self-supervision, Paul (1990) pointed to the significance of critical thinking. More specifically, he emphasized the importance of humility and self-directed learning. In order to provide the best possible service to clients, it is paramount that professionals work toward understanding their limitations. Gibbs and Gambrill (1999) questioned the value of critical thinking and asked whether clients are likely to receive better services if professionals use critical thinking skills. They referred to the extant literature and suggested that caring "is not enough to protect people from harmful practices and to insure that they receive helpful services" (p. 5). They went on to list errors that may occur as a result of incomplete or inaccurate professional perspectives, such as those listed in Table 4.5.

As counselors succumb to internal and external pressure to *solve* client problems and dilemmas, they risk forging ahead without thinking about what drives their decisions and the potential consequences associated with their actions. A common example that frequently surfaces with counselors

---

TABLE 4.4. Critical Thinking Versus Uncritical Thinking

Critical Thinking

a. The art of thinking about your thinking while you're thinking so as to make your thinking more clear, precise, accurate, relevant, consistent, and fair
b. The art of constructive criticism
c. The art of identifying and removing bias, prejudice, and one-sidedness of thought
d. The art of self-directed, in-depth, rational learning
e. Thinking that rationally certifies what we know and makes clear that of which we are ignorant

Uncritical Thinking

a. Thought captive of one's ego, desires, social conditioning, prejudices, or irrational impressions
b. Thinking that is egocentric, careless, and heedless of assumptions, relevant evidence, implications, or consistency
c. Thinking that habitually ignores epistemological demands in favor of its egocentric commitments

Paul, copyright 1990 in *Critical Thinking: What every person needs to survive in a rapidly changing world.* Reprinted with permission of the Foundation for Critical Thinking.

TABLE 4.5. Potential Counselor Errors

- Misclassifying clients
- Continuing intervention too long
- Focusing on irrelevant factors
- Selecting weak intervention methods (e.g., offering psychological counseling when clients need material resources)
- Increasing client dependency
- Overlooking client assets
- Describing behavior unrelated to its context
- Withdrawing intervention too soon
- Not arranging for the generalization and maintenance of positive gains

---

Gibbs and Gambrill, copyright 1999 in *Critical Thinking for Social Workers: Exercises for the helping professions*. Reprinted with permission from Sage Publications, Inc.

surrounds misdiagnosis and inappropriate treatment. By reacting to first impressions and neglecting to critically think about clients and their unique circumstances, counselors can misinterpret vital information and diagnose prematurely. When queried about their decision-making process, counselors are rarely able to describe how they arrived at their conclusion.

According to Irving and Williams (1995), counselors may not be aware of the theories that inform their actions. In fact, when asked to reflect on their practice or elaborate on an intervention, counselors may experience difficulty in identifying their underlying assumptions. Irving and Williams reported that in such situations counselors "say what they believe they are doing rather than what they are actually doing" (p. 108).

In discussing this issue, Irving and Williams (1995) drew on the earlier work of Argyris (1976) and distinguished between theories-in-use and espoused theories. Simply put, *theories-in-use* are a compilation microtheories that allow people to respond to various daily situations. Theories-in-use are comparable to language in daily activities, and they enable people to function without being consciously aware of their use. In essence, they maintain a sense of constancy and provide a predictable worldview. Because theories-in-use are out of an individual's awareness, however, people can perform ineffectively without knowing why.

Despite ongoing difficulties and conflict surrounding particular themes, on an unconscious level people firmly adhere to theories-in-use and are unable to expose them for critical examination. Since it is unlikely that counselors can access their implicit theories-in-use, they can only construct these theories from their actions and statements. In short, people cannot discuss that of which they are unaware.

Espoused theory, on the other hand, refers to stated objectives, claims, what counselors think they are doing, and the sense they are making from their own behavior. However, Argyris (1976) contended, "few people

are aware that the theories they espouse are not the theories they use"
(p. 639). He asserted that people are blind to the discrepancy between
their espoused theories and their theories-in-use because (a) they are
programmed with theories-in-use that do not encourage reflection on
behavior and its impact and (b) people generally do not tell each other
when their espoused theories and theories-in-use are incongruent. This
latter point underscores the potential usefulness of the Johari window
during the process of self-discovery. Counselors who are invested in personal growth can invite colleagues and clients to remark on the congruency
of their philosophical beliefs and behaviors. Professionals who espouse a
constructivist or postmodern approach to counseling, for example, are
often criticized when they assume an educational or directive role in their
work. In essence, these professionals know the postmodern language and
appear to agree with it in principle. However, when it comes down to
actually working with clients, these espoused beliefs seem to dissipate
and there is obvious incongruence between what they say and how they
behave.

☐ Teasing Out Personal Assumptions

To assist counselors in deconstructing their work and identifying underlying assumptions, Irving and Williams (1995) suggested two methods.
The first was a ladder of inference that was proposed by Argyris, Putnam,
and Smith (1987), and the second was a technique to analyze patterns of
interventions and outcomes over time.

The ladder of inference was designed to help professionals "take a question about the counselling process, develop it one step further, then another step, and then yet another step to expose the beliefs and assumptions
underlying it" (Irving and Williams, 1995, p. 113). The progression of the
ladder includes the following steps:

Step 1. Observable counselor behavior
    Example: Providing a client with a home telephone number and
    inviting the client to call at any time.
Step 2: The meanings culturally imposed by a counselor on the behavior
    Questions: Why did I do that? What did I hope to achieve by
    providing the client with my home telephone number and an
    open invitation to call?
Step 3: The meanings a counselor imposes on the cultural meanings of
    the behavior
    Question: What was it about my expected outcome that I valued?

Step 4: The counselor's underlying assumptions.
Questions: What assumptions am I making here? What beliefs do these depend upon?

Irving and Williams (1995) contended that for effective reflective practice, counselors cannot remain within their espoused theory wherein they both deny and defend their assumptions and beliefs. It was their opinion that counselors have to go beyond this superficial level to make explicit and reveal to themselves their theories-in-use.

The second technique focused on analyzing patterns of interventions and outcomes over time and involved a meta-analysis of perceived success or failure. To conduct this process, counselors reviewed their work, identified clients who were considered challenging, and tried to determine common traits among these clients. Once this initial process was completed, recurring patterns were questioned (e.g., What alternative approaches and/or interventions might have been possible? Why weren't any of these chosen?). Irving and Williams (1995) posited that underlying assumptions and theories-in-use can be exposed once counselors recognize patterns and discrepancies in the analysis of various interventions in different situations.

☐ The Mentoring Process

Mentorship can be defined as a close interpersonal relationship between professionals who are at different stages in their professional development (Collins, 1993). Collins described the mentoring process in the following way:

> The mentor—the senior, more professionally advanced of the two—becomes involved in fostering the development and facilitating the advancement of the mentee—the junior professional—by serving as a source of support beyond what is required solely on the basis of their formal role relationship. (p. 123)

Tentoni (1995) provided an excellent review of the counselor mentoring process. He suggested that new graduate counselors expressed feelings of incompetence, were unable to translate their knowledge into the workplace, and had self-doubts. To assist counselors in becoming reflective, a bridge needs to be coconstructed between counselors who are experienced in the reflective process and colleagues who are interested in engaging in this practice.

It would be unrealistic to assume that all relationships that exist between advanced and junior counselors will develop into close and collaborative ones. The interpersonal closeness inherent in a true mentoring relationship develops over time and is predicated on mutual respect and caring. Creating a valuable mentoring relationship involves energy and commitment from both sides. Mentors demonstrate an interest in the well-being of mentees and are sincerely invested in their personal and professional development. For their part, mentees value and respect the experience of more experienced colleagues.

Obviously, there is no correct way to reflect. Nevertheless, different models can be demonstrated that counselors can consider.

Case Vignette

As part of their team supervision, a group of counselors from a community mental health clinic would invite a visiting supervisor to observe their live work with clients and provide feedback. The team consisted of both experienced counselors and recent graduates. Having been through the process several times, the more experienced counselors appreciated how anxious their less experienced colleagues became when it was their time to interview a client in front of an audience of peers as well as a visiting supervisor. To alleviate and normalize the situation as much as possible, the more experienced counselors would agree to present cases first and demonstrate various ways to accept and reflect on feedback. Their intention was to illustrate the value of hearing and integrating different perspectives in a nonthreatening environment. Their leadership set an example and created a path for their less experienced colleagues.

Stickel and Trimmel (1994) indicated the importance of mentoring and noted how this process serves as a necessary bridge between theory and on-the-job demands. Having someone who is willing to enter into a reflective mode, risk vulnerability, and invite feedback from colleagues and clients is invaluable. Mentors can be especially useful to beginning counselors or counselors who fear attack or criticism. Unfortunately, while in graduate school or in practice, some counselors have had their work ridiculed by peers or by their supervisors. These individuals often speak about their past trauma and their reluctance to expose their ideas and work. Sadly, these professionals associate collegial feedback with pain and humiliation.

A number of issues arise regarding mentorship, including dependency, intimacy, conflict, and termination. Each issue has its own set of challenges that needs to be resolved between counselors. Both mentors and mentees can contribute to a sense of dependency. Mentors who insist on remaining central and hovering over less experienced colleagues can contribute to a sense of apprehension and self-doubt within the mentee. In turn, as mentees question their each and every move, they look to their mentors for direction and approval. Rather than work toward professional individuation, both counselors become entangled in a web of mutual dependency.

It is very natural for people to become emotionally close, particularly when they rely on each other for support, confirmation, and professional validation. This might be especially true for counselors who listen to and share traumatic stories and events. There have been instances where mentors and mentees have become infatuated with one another. As they risk and share together, a mutual admiration may develop, and both counselors begin to lose sight of professional boundaries. As with any professional relationship, it is imperative that boundaries and roles be clarified. If not monitored appropriately, counselors may find themselves in precarious situations wherein intimacy causes the lines between their personal and professional lives to be blurred. To prevent unfortunate transgressions from occurring, it becomes the responsibility of both professionals to remain vigilant, to discuss their relationship, and to seek third party consultation when necessary.

The mentor-mentee relationship may not always be smooth and can experience periods of conflict. Orzek (1984) remarked that, "The two basic impulses to manage are aggression and sex. The potential mentee will need to be aware of prioritizing between sexual/romantic feelings, and career issues at certain points in their lives" (p. 74). To ensure that unresolved conflict is not acted out in treatment, counselors need to formulate a plan at the outset of their relationship. Anticipating and celebrating differences of opinion can alleviate anxiety and tension. Moreover, the welcoming of differences is congruent with an underlying principle of reflectivity.

Finally, mentors and mentees need to anticipate the natural evolution of their relationship and its eventual termination. As they grow and develop together, mentees begin to demonstrate autonomy and self-reliance, while mentors seek new challenges. Although the period of separation can be predicted, it is not always easy. Some counselors celebrate and ritualize this process, while others are unsure of how to move the relationship to a different level. Professionals who struggle with terminating their relationship may find it helpful to seek consultation from peers or an outside party.

☐ Conclusion

Reflective practice can be a useful process for counselors. As they reflect on their personhood and practice, counselors become more familiar with themselves, are less likely to project personal issues onto clients, and are more likely to entertain multiple perspectives. Although this process can be exhilarating and rewarding, it is also laden with potential for anxiety and defensiveness. The reflection process takes time, patience, and courage. Although it would be presumptuous to think that only seasoned counselors possess the capacity to reflect, perhaps clinical experience does play an important role in appreciating the need for reflectivity. Over time counselors begin to understand the unpredictability and complexity of their work. They realize that there are no set formulas for cases, even those that appear similar to each other. Each case is unique and will affect counselors in different ways.

The process of questioning long-held assumptions, beliefs, and values entails elements of open-mindedness, wholeheartedness, and intellectual responsibility. Regardless of how counselors choose to reflect, these aforementioned principles are necessary and underpin the self-examination process. Finally, for some counselors, reflection can occur naturally and spontaneously. For others, mentoring may assist them in becoming acquainted with purpose and methods.

This chapter has provided questions and processes designed to assist professionals who are interested in embarking on this journey of self-discovery. Hopefully, as the self-supervision becomes further articulated, counselors will develop additional questions and processes that can be used for their own personal and professional growth. A consequence of such professional integrity and rigor will be enhanced client welfare.

☐ Review/Discussion Questions

1. What are some potential advantages associated with reflective thinking?
2. What are some potential roadblocks to reflective thinking?
3. Describe the developmental framework for reflective thinking.
4. Describe the purpose of critical thinking.
5. What is the purpose of mentoring during the self-reflection process?

5

Self-Supervision in Action

Self-supervision is deliberate thinking about one's actions, independent of others. This evaluative or reflective activity is performed to better understand how we operate as therapists and/or supervisors and to offer opportunities to take a different view or position in the clinical context.

—Diane Steiden, 1993

A formalized and systematic process of self-supervision involves more than an invitation to consider the therapeutic process and its overall context. In reality, self-supervision is a complex endeavor that moves beyond a general discernment and encompasses (a) introspection, (b) self-awareness, and (c) self-evaluation culminating in enhanced counselor insight, skill, and functioning. To achieve these goals, counselors need to assume an active self-regulating role to evaluate their professional development. Consequently, they become responsible for their clinical decisions and actions and remain individually accountable.

Self-supervision can be utilized by a variety of helping professionals at various levels of development. Fundamental requirements would include (a) a basic understanding of interpersonal communication, (b) reasonable insight into the counseling process, (c) self-initiation, and (d) a willingness to become vulnerable while exploring personal strengths and needs. Implementation scheduled at particular developmental stages, however, would be inappropriate in that it presupposes a correlation between counselor progress and the ability to accurately self-monitor. As alluded to earlier, some novice counselors might illustrate a greater capacity to self-supervise than colleagues with more clinical experience. What needs to be emphasized are the skills required for counselors to (a) objectively reflect on their work, (b) identify and extract significant data, (c) process the extracted data, and (d) effectively integrate what they have learned from their reflections. In essence, counselors who see their development as a process and realize the complexity of the situations they encounter along the way appreciate self-supervision. Because of the variety of personalities and clinical problems counselors typically encounter, it becomes even more important that they carefully consider their work.

☐ Information Gathering and Integration

Though it sounds straightforward, self-supervision is a rigorous and complex process that can encompass a great deal of information. During this process, counselors begin to bring together information from different sources. For example, self-supervising counselors must consider information about their relationships with clients, information about themselves (past and present) in relation to clients, and finally, new information that results from reflection on this information. Being able to combine parts or all aspects of the self-supervision process (e.g., audio- or videotape review components, clinical notes, client-family feedback) into a working model that improves treatment takes time and experience.

Self-supervision involves personal reflection leading to a deliberation process that entails drawing the present clinical situation into focus in a broad perspective that includes both past experiences and future potentials. It can also be considered a valuable preventative procedure or a way to lessen the probability of unfortunate incidences occurring in treatment (e.g., ethical violations, counselor-client conflict, burnout). When counselors are uncertain about a particular situation, turning to a self-supervision model may help them to consider options and alternatives.

☐ The Timing of Self-Supervision

Regardless of their experience and skill level, counselors are encouraged to reflect on issues that effect their work and clinical outcomes. Counselors can begin to learn the basic elements of self-supervision by first identifying and recording personal reactions during counseling. The exercise is intended to help counselors become sensitive to minor changes in their mood or behavior. For example, counselors might notice that although they started a session enthusiastically, they became pessimistic over the course of the interview. Simply noticing this type of mood change is important.

The next step in their self-supervision might include reflecting on these reactions and mood changes during an audio- or videotape review of the interview. Emphasis at this stage is placed on connecting personal reactions with certain turning points (e.g., a child cursing at a parent, a client leaving the interview abruptly) or clinical themes (e.g., death, chronic illness). This phase can demonstrate that, without their awareness, counselors can be affected by events within an interview. It can also prompt counselors to think about how personal issues can be perturbed and reactivated by client statements or behaviors.

Increased counselor expectations may follow with more experience and interest. For example, counselors might search for deeper connections between themes that emerge in treatment with personal issues (e.g., sexuality, violence, abandonment, etc.). What needs to be underscored when embarking on self-supervision is the importance of noticing personal reactions (either physiological or emotional). Rather than dismissing and ignoring subtle personal reactions, self-supervising counselors remain sensitive and consider the implications associated with their experiences. In one case, a counselor who was annoyed with a client for arriving late for an interview dismissed his reaction as normal, insignificant, and transitory. As the interview progressed, however, he noticed that his unresolved anger toward the client lingered and was affecting the way in which he was responding to the client (e.g., uncharacteristic quips). In addition to underestimating his unresolved anger, the counselor failed to consider how his emotional disposition would effect the therapeutic process. Self-supervising counselors pay special attention to such emotional indicators.

☐ Participation in the Self-Supervisory Process

Self-supervision can actually include a variety of people. According to Todd (1997b), "Self-supervision does not have to be a solitary process. It can include the use of peers or less formal resources such as spouses or friends, assuming that confidentiality is not breached" (p. 24). Disclosing and discussing salient issues, however, generally requires a certain amount of trust between the counselors and those with whom they are sharing their work. A distinction is drawn here between discussing professional growth issues with individuals we trust and formal consultation. The former process generally involves revealing personal information and insights to gain additional feedback from significant others.

☐ Development of Counselor Self-Reliance

At times, personal behaviors and patterns, which are outside of a counselor's awareness, are pointed out and can be linked to therapeutic work. At these moments, the thread that weaves between the counselor's personal life and clinical practice becomes evident. Regardless of the context, what needs to be carefully considered when promoting self-supervision is the difficulty professionals experience in moving away from a traditional supervisory format, which is usually conducted in a top-down fashion (Neufeldt, 1997). Inviting counselors to develop self-confidence and to rely on personal instincts and skills can be a challenge and a major developmental step. Counselors often miss the security that was offered by supervisors during graduate school. The notion of stepping out on their own and relying on their own instincts can be intimidating.

When closely scrutinized, the skills that are needed to self-supervise become more apparent. These skills are inexorably tied to a preoccupation with the therapeutic process, skill acquisition, and performance anxiety. Teyber (1992) contended that although it is relatively easy to see the reenactment of a client's conflicts in his or her interpersonal process, it can be exasperatingly difficult to recognize one's own interpersonal process while in an intense, affect-laden relationship. Thus, counselors must exercise patience and realize that the ability to recognize and respond at the process level is acquired slowly. It seems only reasonable that counselors will require ample time to acclimatize before feeling confident about entering into a self-monitoring mode. The duration of this period will depend upon the unique circumstances of each professional and how valuable he or she finds the process.

☐ Perceptual, Conceptual, and Executive Skills

A focus on perceptual, conceptual, and executive skills as outlined by Tomm and Wright (1979) provides counselors with a workable framework from which to initially self-supervise. Briefly, perceptual and conceptual skills refer to what is taking place in the mind of the counselor and form the basis for his or her overt actions. More specifically, perceptual skills refer to the ability to make accurate observations, conceptual skills refer to the ability to attribute meaning to clinical observations, and executive skills refer to the affective response and counselor overt intervention. While reflecting on a session and reviewing their clinical notes or audio- or videotapes, counselors can consider the aforementioned aspects of their work. Obviously, the development of specific skills will hinge on their theoretical orientation and individual needs. For example, counselors who are interested in maintaining a systemic framework in treatment may focus on a tendency to drift toward viewing the aggressive behavior of children in isolation rather than in a larger context. During the self-supervision process, such counselors might consider the various factors that contributing to their shifting conceptualization and emerging reductionist perspective. In other words, what client behavior(s) is influencing the counselor and contribute to a shift in his or her thinking? Commonly, counselors who claim to be systemically oriented begin describing clients in reductionist terms when treatment does not go as planned. These professionals, for example, move away from describing interactional patterns and begin to speak about chemical imbalances and biological etiologies. The point being made here has nothing to do with a professional's theoretical preference, but rather with the need for professionals to reflect on their reactions and clinical decisions.

☐ Pragmatics of Self-Supervision

In spite of the implicit intricacies that encompass self-supervision, minimal attention has been rendered to the finer details of this process and to the skills necessary to achieve proficiency in self-reflection, extraction, and integration. Bernard and Goodyear (1992) emphasized that the intensity inherent in the self-supervision process is designed to fine-tune both case conceptualization and personal knowledge. The exact way in which counselors are taught to monitor their work remains vague, and therefore is vulnerable to ongoing confusion and misunderstanding (Langs, 1979; Todd, 1992). Common assumptions, for example, are that counselors possess the natural ability to self-supervise, evolve into a self-supervision mode, or arrive at the ability to self-supervise by chance.

To enhance the self-supervision process, careful consideration needs to be rendered to eventual implementation. Thus, the fundamental and immediate questions of who, what, when, where, and how emerge. Since it cannot be assumed that every counselor has the ability or the necessary preparation to embark on this arduous process, a number of fundamental steps are recommended and are discussed below. Although not imperative, the following ideas are suggested as ways to set the stage and augment the self-supervision process.

Alternatives, Curiosity, and Generalizations

Remaining curious and open-minded while involved in the practice of brainstorming ideas and alternatives is essential during self-supervision

(Todd, 1997b). This practice can promote self-discovery and personal empowerment (e.g., Amundson, Stewart, & Valentine, 1993; Cecchin, Lane, & Ray, 1992; 1993). Williams (1995) described the establishment of a *wisdom culture*, wherein an intersubjective space is created and "knowing and doubting are balanced; ignorance is dangerous, but so is knowledge, *if that knowledge* [italics in original] is narrowly specialist" (p. 212). To become less rigid and more curious, counselors are encouraged to slow down the therapeutic process and focus on client narratives and personal reactions. Counselors should be less interested in solving client problems and more interested in the role they assume in counseling and their reactions during counseling.

Some counselors, however, due to their adherence to a specific theoretical conceptualization, may face the additional challenge of becoming less orthodox, more creative, and more flexible in their work (Haley, 1996). This usually entails challenging ingrained beliefs about one's self, one's clients, and the change process. As noted earlier, Henson-Matthews and Marshall (1988) suggested that professionals who demonstrated high self-monitoring skills were more flexible and endorsed multiple therapeutic approaches as compared to low self-monitors, who gravitated to a single theoretical approach. Counselors are encouraged to color outside the lines and challenge conventional wisdom and protocol. Cecchin et al. (1992) agreed that counselors' enthusiasm for a model or hypothesis could help them get close to clients, even while they maintained their curiosity and respect. These authors further contended that,

> it is at the moment when the therapist begins to reflect upon the effect of his own attitude and presumptions that he acquires a position that is both ethical and therapeutic. In order to be able to attain this ability for self-reflexivity, we believe that it is necessary to have a certain level of irreverence and a sense of humor, which one acquires by maintaining a continuous conversation with colleagues, people outside the mental health field, students, and patients alike. (p. 9)

In assuming an irreverent position, counselors can avoid taking a specific model too seriously. As a result, they can embrace uncertainty, become playful, and consider new ideas and beliefs.

Audio- and Videotape Reviews

Reviewing audio- and videotapes of their work can be invaluable during the self-supervising process. While doing so, counselors can pay careful attention to, and make note of, aspects of the interview that they find rewarding or disconcerting. In both cases, counselors can attempt to identify personal reactions, which they recall from the interview, or what was being said that affected them personally. Haber (1996) suggested several overriding questions that professionals might ask themselves when assuming a metaview during the self-supervision process, including, "What generates your concern about the interview?"; "Why do you think you intervened in this manner?"; and "Why do you think you and the family would respond to the suggested interventions?" Because self-supervision can be challenging, the development of specific questions can serve as a guiding framework during audio or video review.

Connecting Notes With Corresponding Tape Segments

Having clinical notes available, along with the corresponding audio- or videotape, can provide counselors with valuable information upon which to ponder and reflect. At this point, counselors can begin to articulate their reactions and therapeutic dilemmas or breakthroughs. With substantial information at hand, counselors can begin to entertain different clinical perspectives and treatment alternatives.

Inviting Client Feedback

Counselors can invite clients to share their impressions of the therapeutic process. This strategy can be useful to counselors and an empowering experience for clients. When using this specific strategy, counselors regularly ask clients how they perceive the progress of treatment and whether defined goals are being achieved. Counselors have reported the value in this process for several reasons, including (a) helping them form a respectful and collaborative relationship with clients, (b) opening up counselor-client communication and rapport, and (c) helping them remain focused on clinical objectives and clinical outcome. Todd (1997b) noted that "Clients may need encouragement to be truthful and reassurance that their feedback will help their therapy be more to them" (p. 22). In short, client feedback can provide counselors with valuable information, which they can consider and contrast with their existing perceptions.

Before clients disclose information that can benefit the counseling process, however, it is essential that a trusting relationship be established and maintained. It is unlikely that clients will reveal their opinions if they feel that their comments or suggestions will be perceived as insults or if they fear counselor retaliation. For clients to fully participate, counselors need to first gain their confidence by demonstrating maturity, genuine interest, and professionalism. Counselors should remain mindful that many clients are unaccustomed to being asked for their feedback; therefore, they may need to be gradually introduced to this collaborative process. Although agreeing at first, clients may remain hesitant in expressing their true feelings. To assist clients, counselors may need to periodically ask for feedback and demonstrate a positive response. The format in which feedback is shared depends on client preference. One colleague for example, encouraged a client to express her opinions regarding the counseling process in a letter.

☐ Self-Supervision: Preliminary Guidelines

A substantial degree of individual responsibility underlies counselor self-supervision. Personal reflection demands concentration. To notice personal idiosyncrasies as well as subtle counselor-client interactions, professionals need to remain focused and attentive. For effective self-supervision, counselors need to organize their material within a manageable framework. Counselors may not know what to look for while reviewing their clinical notes or audio- and videotaped sessions, or how to organize information once it is extracted. To assist in the review process, a series of questions that counselors can ponder are included in Table 5.1. While considering the information that emerges from these questions, counselors can attempt to identify and consider personal issues that effect their work.

To effectively self-supervise, counselors are expected to step back from their work, become introspective, and reflect on overt and covert responses that influence their interactions with clients. This process typically involves careful and intentional review of audio- and videotapes; detailed clinical notes; and documentation of personal experiences, usually in the form of autobiographies or journals. Video-assisted self-monitoring provides feedback as counselors are able to confront themselves on tape, adjust their behavior, and develop confidence in the ability to respond to

---

TABLE 5.1. Potential Review Process Questions

1. Why am I feeling so responsible for this client?
2. How have I become so invested in this client?
3. What specific client system characteristics am I reacting to?
4. Is there a central theme that triggers a negative or positive response in me?
5. What outside pressures are influencing my work?
6. Why is it so important for me to succeed with this case?
7. How did I feel before, during, and after the session (e.g., disappointed, hopeful, excited, frightened)? Why?
8. What did I like or dislike about my interactions with the client?
9. What am I experiencing emotionally and physically as I think about this case?

clients in a helpful manner. During the intentional review process, counselors identify issues (either positive or negative) that merit closer inspection, and emphasis is placed on mobilizing counselor resources through increased self-knowledge.

The following focus areas have been developed to provide a preliminary guide to self-supervision: intrapersonal, interpersonal, and clinical. Associated with each focus area is an objective(s) that details its purpose, a rationale that explains why it is important to work toward meeting the objective, and finally, practical strategies that can be employed to meet the objective. Presenting a sample case will help to demonstrate the applicability of practical strategies.

Case Vignette

Philip and Wendy requested an appointment at a child guidance center for help with their 15-year-old daughter, Betsy. It was mentioned on the intake form that Betsy was an only child exhibiting adolescent tantrums and an unwillingness to follow parental directives.

After exchanging pleasantries and confirming demographic information during the first few minutes of the initial interview, Nancy began to engage the parents in a conversation about their concerns. Shortly after beginning to express their concerns, Betsy interrupted and refused to allow her parents an opportunity to identify their concerns. Each time they tried to speak, Betsy would make a snide remark or an annoying sound. In response, both parents took turns reprimanding Betsy. Despite numerous parental and counselor attempts to reassure Betsy that she would have equal time to express herself, she remained oppositional.

In an attempt to manage the interview and institute some order, Nancy eventually asked to speak to both parents alone. Although opposed to the idea, Betsy grudgingly agreed to sit in the waiting room. While speaking with the parents, Nancy was insistent that they had to begin establishing effective boundaries by presenting a united front and demanding that their daughter respect them by remaining quiet while they spoke. If Betsy defied her parents, a consequence would have to follow. Nancy presented her idea in a confident manner and reassured the parents that it was the best plan of action.

When the family interview resumed, Betsy immediately wanted to know what was said during the private conversation. Nancy informed the youngster that the conversation was private and that both parents had something to say. On Nancy's cue, Philip informed his daughter that he and his wife would no longer tolerate her belligerent and rude behavior and would set a consequence if necessary. Even before Philip could finish, however, Betsy began to question Nancy's experience and intentions. In a dramatic fashion she stood up, glared at Nancy, and questioned her competency. Unprepared for such criticism, Nancy became quite sullen and appeared uncertain.

After a few seconds, but what seemed like hours, Nancy tried to regain her composure. Both parents were obviously sympathetic towards Nancy. In an attempt to support Nancy, Philip commented that Betsy's dramatic performance and contemp-

tuous behavior was typical. After marking her ground and upping the ante, Betsy returned to her seat and appeared pleased with her conquest.

Feeling quite disoriented and emotionally shaken, Nancy began discussing the storm and stress of adolescence and how much time behavioral change can take. In reality, Nancy was unsure of what to do and was hoping that the session time would pass quickly. Shortly before the interview ended, Philip and Wendy reiterated the gravity of the situation and suggested that perhaps a male counselor could help.

Intrapersonal Aspect of the Interview

Objective 1

The first objective purpose of this focus area is to identify and understand the significance of personal emotions and feelings during an interview. Common counselor emotions include:

- disappointment (e.g., when a client reports that a prescribed intervention did not result in an anticipated outcome),
- relief (e.g., when a desired client behavioral change is reported),
- fear (e.g., when a client threatens self-harm),
- anxiety (e.g., when a client inquires about a counselor's clinical experience), and
- anger (e.g., when a client fails to follow through on a homework assignment).

Rationale

It is important that counselors understand how their personal emotions and feelings can systemically impact the counseling process. Being fearful, for example, can effectively paralyze counselors and reduce their clinical maneuverability. Correspondingly, clients who sense counselor fear or hesitancy are unlikely to follow therapeutic suggestions with confidence. Hackney and Cormier (1996) elaborated, "Self-awareness and understanding also contribute to greater security and safety for both counselor and client. Lack of self-awareness and understanding may cause some counselors to personalize or over-react to client messages and respond with defensiveness" (p. 16). Rather than assuming that emotions are simply transitory, counselors are encouraged to carefully reflect on the meaning and potential influence of their emotions.

Practical Strategies

- It is important to create a relaxing and quiet environment, prior to or following an interview, that is conducive to introspection. Counselor reflection should occur with minimal interruptions in order to remain focused and attentive. Attempting to focus in an environment that is disruptive or noisy only defeats the purpose of trying to concentrate and track physical and emotional reactions experienced during counseling.

- Energy needs to be directed toward personal awareness, needs, and growth as opposed to problem solving. Rather than thinking about clinical interventions, the reflective period can be perceived as a time of self-centeredness. During this time, counselors focus on personal needs rather than client needs. The premise underlying this strategy is that counselors need to work toward gaining an understanding of self before attempting to understand and stabilize others. In the preceding case vignette, the counselor experienced emotions warranting examination. Why did the youngster's flippant remarks strike a cord in the counselor? Was there some truth to the remarks? What other client comments could effectively paralyze the counselor and prevent her from doing her job effectively? Questions abound when focusing on self. It becomes a private time wherein professionals move from behind their professional degrees and reflect on personal insecurities, fears, and anxieties.

  Remaining focused on self rather than clinical goals and interventions can be a challenge. Having been trained and conditioned to assess client needs and develop appropriate clinical goals, counselors may experience difficulty assuming what appears to be a self-centered position. Influenced by their own anxiety about helping clients, counselors worry about what to do next rather than about who they are and how they are reacting. Counselor educators who encourage students to remain focused on client needs are unlikely to invite students to become introspective. A recent research finding indicated that marriage and family therapy students identified their best supervisory experiences occurred in contexts where there was a balance between personal growth with the development of technical skills. Conversely, poor supervisory experiences tended to involve an emphasis of technical skills over personal growth (Anderson, Schlossberg, & Rigazio-DiGilio, 2000). This finding supported earlier discoveries regarding the experiences of psychology students.

- It is fundamental that counselors appreciate the importance of self-care and realize that self-supervision is a time for self-development and, ultimately, improved service delivery. During self-supervision, the psychological health of counselors is given high priority, and the important connection between counselor well-being and competent service delivery is underscored. Although counselor self-care is addressed in more detail in Chapter 6, this issue cannot be overemphasized. When considering how vulnerable counselors are in transgressing boundaries, special attention should be devoted to this issue.

- A careful review of issues or incidents (triggering events) should be conducted from clinical notes that were personally meaningful. It becomes important that counselors complete their notations as quickly as possible following interviews to ensure accurate descriptions. Although counselors commonly believe that they will be able to recall important information, experience teaches them otherwise. Recording the intensity of emotions can be particularly helpful for later review. Following the course of a day, and after different clinical experiences, counselors may experience difficulty in recalling their emotions during a specific interview.

Case Vignette (continued)

After the interview with Philip, Wendy, and Betsy ended, Nancy immediately returned to her office, closed her door, and was whirling from a myriad of emotions. She tried to scribble some notes but was still fuming. She was angry with Betsy for flaring up, questioning her competency, and embarrassing her in front of Philip and Wendy. Her irritation increased when she thought about how wrong Betsy was to even question her expertise. After all, she did have a master's degree, postgraduate training at an internationally recognized institute, and experience.

Nancy was also feeling extremely frustrated with Philip and Wendy for their inability to raise their child. She wondered how parents could let a young person become so powerful and forceful. She resented the fact that parents like Philip and Wendy expected professionals to work with situations that had deteriorated to such alarming degrees. Fleetingly, Nancy was also annoyed with herself for not knowing how to help the family. When feelings of personal disappointment seeped in, however, she followed her normal routine of quickly deflecting her feelings of inferiority onto her clients.

After allowing herself time to emotionally vent, Nancy took her telephone off the hook and tried to focus on what was going on with her, rather than with her clients. As she proceeded, she identified her anger, shame, and disappointment.

Objective 2

Once a feeling or emotion has been identified, counselors need to begin articulating the possible origin of positive or negative feelings experienced before, during, or after an interview. Instead of holding clients responsible for how counselors feel, counselors can slowly trace their reactions to specific events in their lives.

Rationale. Following the recognition and acknowledgment of meaningful issues, counselors can work toward tracking corresponding feelings that are associated with these issues to their possible origins. This process can provide counselors with valuable information about self and others. For example, feelings of sadness that cloud a counselor's work in cases of marital separation may be connected to personal issues of abandonment or loss. Simply dismissing such feelings as symptoms of a bad day, for example, ignores unresolved personal issues that affect therapeutic interactions. Anticipating triggering events prior to interviews that typically arouse personal emotions can prepare counselors and assist them in conducting interviews.

It is understood that this exercise may not be practical for counselors who work in emergency or walk-in settings. Counselors who work in such unique settings may not have the luxury of pondering clinical notes prior to meeting a client. Nevertheless, as these professionals enter into a counseling session they can remain cognizant that it is inevitable that issues will arise that will effect their interactions with clients.

Practical Strategies.

- Reflect on past or current issues that may be triggered during counseling and influence one's clinical work. For example, clients who appear disheveled or who practice certain behavioral habits can trigger unpleasant memories and stimulate a negative counselor response, thus jeopardizing the therapeutic relationship.
- Begin constructing a personal genogram, timeline, and autobiography. These exercises can be helpful in remembering and organizing significant events.
- Review personal family history and patterns.

Case Vignette (continued)

Nancy remembered similar social and professional situations where she had felt belittled after her competence was called into question. She had always considered herself a good person and a hard worker, and she believed that the perceived attacks against her were cruel and unjustified. Nevertheless, she took comments to heart and secretly questioned their validity. Just thinking about previous episodes made her blush and become defensive. She desperately wanted these feelings to disappear, but they lingered. There was a part of Nancy that just wanted to quit and leave the helping profession entirely—the pain she was experiencing just wasn't worth it.

As she sat alone in her office, Nancy gradually calmed down and recounted occasions throughout her life when she felt attacked and humiliated. Recounting instances and recalling haunting memories was not difficult. For example, there was the time in middle school when her coach scolded her during a basketball game. She vividly remembered returning to the team bench, feeling humiliated and hurt. Then there was the unforgettable family wedding where her cousins publicly laughed at and teased her for dancing with a boy. Also, how could she ever forget the landscaping foreman at her summer job who sarcastically suggested that she seek an occupation more suitable for a woman? Finally, there was the unforgettable time in graduate school when her supervisor made a disparaging remark about her age and lack of clinical experience in front of her supervision group. As she relived these unfortu-

nate situations, Nancy found herself flooding with emotion, getting very warm, and clenching the arms of her chair. Although long past, these events were still very much alive for her and had surfaced as Betsy confronted her. Philip and Wendy's look of non-confidence had further fueled her feelings of humiliation and incompetence.

As she reflected, Nancy was quite surprised by the power and similarity of these events. She was curious as to why she had fallen into a pattern of taking comments about her competence so seriously, especially from people who held little meaning in her life. The incident with Betsy and her family wasn't the first time Nancy had responded negatively to a client's remarks. She realized that her pattern involved withdrawing emotionally from clients, harboring anger toward them, and retreating to nurse her psychological wounds.

Objective 3

The purpose of this objective is to work toward resolving issues through traditional supervision, consultation, or personal counseling.

Rationale. The need for conventional supervision, consultation, or personal counseling may be required when professionals are unable to resolve personal issues that recur and continue to impede their work with clients. Personal supervision, consultation, or counseling can complement self-supervision and provide counselors with different perspectives from which to consider their dilemmas. According to Corey (1997), in order to enter into the world of clients, counselors should heal their own psychological wounds. He further stated that, "As counselors we can take our clients no further than we have been willing to go in our own life" (p. 19).

Practical Strategies

- In order to resolve personal difficulties, counselors can seek appropriate professional assistance and support. Depending on their specific concern(s) and treatment plan, counselors may be able to continue working with clients. However, if a personal issue(s) can potentially have a negative affect on the therapeutic relationship and client welfare, counselors would be ethically bound to refer clients.
- Review additional relevant educational resources (e.g., readings, training audio- or videotapes, workshops).

Case Vignette (continued)

Although she had read and attended numerous workshops on transference and countertransference and building effective counselor-client relationships, Nancy realized that her current reactions to clients were somehow connected to her need to be accepted and valued by them. She didn't understand why some clients seemed to underestimate her education, training, and experience. She wondered if she presented herself as unprofessional or uncertain. The more she thought about it, the more she recognized a deep need to be acknowledged and respected as a professional. It became clear to her that whenever her ability was questioned, she would be startled, offended, and eventually retreat in self-doubt.

Due to her pride, Nancy was hesitant to discuss these experiences with her supervisor. When queried about her cases, Nancy would skillfully avoid discussing concerns about being intimidated and describe events as challenging and interesting. She knew, however, that something had to be done or similar situations would surely be repeated. The challenge was finding someone trustworthy to whom she could reveal her insecurities. Having been chastised in the past based on her performance, Nancy felt very vulnerable and was reluctant to reach out for help. The idea of participating in a local supervision group sounded appealing but risky.

Interpersonal Aspect of the Interview

Objective 1

The purpose of this objective is to work toward identifying points in a session where negative or positive feelings may have occurred by reviewing clinical notes and audio- or videotapes (e.g., what was said, what was intimated, nonverbal client behaviors).

Rationale. During this review, focus is placed on identifying critical transitional points where positive or negative feelings emerge. Such transitional points can be revealing to counselors in their interactions with clients. For example, noticing personal irritability when clients ask about the time remaining in an interview may initially appear meaningless but may be highly symbolic for counselors (e.g., counselors assume that clients are losing interest in the session, which leaves the counselor feeling unappreciated or ineffective). Hackney and Cormier (1996) suggested that projection can occur when counselors are unaware of their blind spots. They wrote, "Self-awareness and understanding are important in counseling for a variety of reasons. First they help you see more objectively and avoid *blind spots* [italics in original], that is, difficulties that may arise because you do not understand some aspects of yourself, particularly in interpersonal interactions" (p. 16).

Practical Strategies.

- Identify interpersonal patterns that recur and prove helpful, distracting, or irritating (e.g., clients who continually arrive late for interviews).
- Track behavioral sequences to make connections (e.g., counselor disclosure appears to positively influence the counselor-client relation-

ship, which in turn appears to contribute to overall counselor-client collaboration and cooperativeness).

Case Vignette (continued)

As Nancy replayed the interview in her head, she concluded that initially she was feeling confident and was gaining Philip and Wendy's confidence and respect. During their private conversation, Philip and Wendy appeared convinced of Nancy's diagnosis and action plan. Moreover, she felt in control and supported by the two parents. Things drastically changed, however, when Betsy appeared to see through her and began to challenge her competence. As soon as Betsy raised her voice and went on the attack, Nancy became disoriented and shrank. Was it fear? Was it intimidation? Was it self-doubt? All Nancy knew was that rather than respond to Betsy, she reacted and became very defensive. It was as if Betsy knew exactly which button to push to arouse her insecurities.

Nancy's education, training, and experience seemed meaningless and no match for Betsy. It was as if Betsy touched a nerve that Nancy could not conceal. Reluctantly, she pondered her tendency to base her self-esteem on people's evaluation of her.

Objective 2

The purpose of this objective is to consider relationships with clients.

Rationale. It is highly unlikely that counseling will progress unless a positive relationship has been established, nurtured, and maintained. Therefore, the fundamental principles (e.g., respect, empathy, congruence) underlying the counseling relationship require ongoing attention.

Practical Strategies.

- Review personal behavior and conduct during interactions with clients. For example, are the basic rules of courtesy being followed?
- Review the transition stages of an interview (e.g., social or engagement stage, problem-identification stage, interaction stage, intervention stage, closing stage).

Case Vignette (continued)

To gain a more global perspective on what had transpired, Nancy thought about the relationship she had formed with Betsy. It became clear to her that in reacting to Betsy's behavior, she assumed a parental role, quickly moved to form an alliance with Philip and Wendy, and in the meantime neglected Betsy. Nancy grew frustrated with herself and felt somewhat empathetic toward Betsy, as she thought about how she had raced through the social stage into the problem identification stage without allowing Betsy time to get to know her. In retrospect, Nancy had many questions: Why was it so important for her to rescue the parents from what she perceived to be an embarrassing situation? Why she was so invested in quelling Betsy's disrespectful behavior? Who did Betsy's behavior remind her of? Why did she quickly lose her confidence and retreat when confronted by Betsy? A pattern that was becoming clear to Nancy involved clinical and social situations that challenged her confidence and expertise. She could recall times when she became doubtful about her abilities and skills and would experience elevated discomfort.

Clinical Aspect of the Interview

Objective 1

The purpose of this objective is to separate interview notes and tape(s) into basic perceptual, conceptual, and executive skills.

Rationale. Making the connection that exists among what they observe, how they think about what they observe, and how they respond to what they observe can provide counselors with information about how they proceeded in treatment. Tracking their clinical interventions back to initial observations allows counselors to understand their thinking processes.

Practical Strategies.

- Consider the logical flow regarding what is being observed, the thoughts associated with what is being observed, and interventions that follow.
- Search for counselor skills, strengths, and resources (e.g., which counseling interventions appeared helpful).

Case Vignette (continued)

Nancy began to question why she had become anxious and assumed so much responsibility for Betsy's behavior. Was she invested in having Betsy understand how inconsiderate and hurtful her behavior was? Having been worried that the situation would intensify, Nancy now realized that she had reacted and tried to settle a longstanding problem within a few short minutes. She grinned as she envisioned herself in a superhero uniform swooping down and instantly correcting the family's dilemma. Theoretically, she understood that Philip, Wendy, and Betsy were embroiled in a serious family problem. In the heat of action, however, she seemed to go on autopilot and reacted out of anxiety and fear.

As Nancy gained a greater perspective, she not only saw the humor in her attempt to help the family, but realized that she had, in fact, quickly conceptualized a treatment plan that could potentially help Betsy and her family. In retrospect, a number of problem areas within the interview became clear: (a) her failure to engage Betsy, (b) poor timing in speaking with the parents privately, and (c) being intimidated by a demanding and sensational teenager. Despite these shortcomings, Nancy moved away from thinking in black and white and perceiving the interview as a total disaster. In fact, there were positives.

Objective 2

Remain focused on short-term (in session) and long-term goal achieve-ment and the integration of self-reflection data.

Rationale. To avoid disappointment, while appreciating the rigor and complexity of clinical work, counselors are encouraged to set realistic goals and slowly integrate data that they have discovered during the reflective process. In reality, counseling involves hard work for professionals and clients alike. Counselor self-discipline is required to remain on course; particularly during times of frustration (e.g., clinical relapses). What needs to be reemphasized, however, is that counselor frustration has to do with the person-of-the-counselor and not with clients. Projecting personal frustration onto clients serves no purpose and is likely to culminate in conflict and premature termination. Counselors must be mature enough to accept the good times as well as the more difficult times in their career.

Practical Strategies.

- Focus on the importance of small, incremental gains as well as long-term goals. The tendency for counselors to set unrealistic goals in order to help clients solve their presenting problem(s) quickly can easily backfire. Well-intentioned counselors can respond to the seriousness of client problems by becoming anxious and overzealous. Rather than carefully crafting the course of treatment, unrealistic goals are established. This is not to say that clinical problems that are perceived as serious cannot be resolved in short order. However, counselors would be wise to conduct assessments and monitor the course of treatment carefully.
- Remain specific and focused during self-supervision. Moving from issue to issue can confuse matters and end in frustration. Persistence and patience can be rewarded by new insights and discoveries.
- Identify a specific area upon which to focus to prevent counselors from becoming overwhelmed and disoriented. Attempting to reflect on several issues simultaneously can defeat the purpose of the exercise. For example, focusing on why he or she becomes annoyed when a child interrupts parents when they are speaking in a session can assist the counselor in better understanding his or her failure to maintain a systemic perspective in treatment.
- Gradually connect information from audio- and videotapes, clinical notes, and discussions with colleagues (when available) to actual clini-

cal practice. Being able to actually utilize what is discovered during the reflective process is central to self-supervision. Uncovering a personal pattern is only useful if this information can be integrated into one's work with clients.

Case Vignette (continued)

Perhaps Nancy's greatest findings included becoming aware of her personal vulnerabilities and how these vulnerabilities influenced her interaction with clients, the need to remain aware of personal issues when attempting to engage clients, and the need to set small and realistic goals. Despite the appeal of the long-term goal of having Philip and Wendy establish effective boundaries with their daughter, a great deal of groundwork had to be covered first. By remaining aware of her tendency to feel defensive and shrink under criticism, Nancy could be proactive, utilize various strategies to decrease her discomfort, and continue working with Betsy and her family. For example, when similar situations occurred in the future, Nancy could calmly excuse herself from the interview and take time to consider how she would like to respond. She could also inform the client family that loud and abrasive behaviors were distracting and contributed to her sense of discomfort. Nancy began to understand that she did not have to overhaul her counseling style or preferences to accommodate clients. With negotiation, there could be moderate changes on both sides.

The self-supervision process did not provide Nancy with extraordinary ideas or innovative strategies. It was useful, however, in helping her reflect on personal beliefs, assumptions, and responsibilities. In concrete terms, Nancy *learned about herself.* While reflecting, Nancy began to make connections, from the past to the present, and was beginning to appreciate how these events continued to influence her work. The strategies employed by counselors (genograms, video-reviews, journaling) are left to the discretion of each professional.

☐ Conclusion

The self-supervision process involves the gathering and integration of information that originates from a variety of sources and time frames. As described in this chapter, the impact of historical events can seep into and influence the counseling relationship. At first, the task of managing and synthesizing information can appear daunting. With time and experience, however, this process becomes more natural and is slowly integrated into a clinician's routine. Counselors who are embarking on the self-supervision process can take small steps and gradually enhance their repertoire. The degree to which they immerse themselves in this self-discovery and regulating process will depend on their interest, the value they place on the self-monitoring process, and their needs.

To value self-supervision, counselors need to appreciate how intrapersonal, interpersonal, and clinical aspects of a counseling interview effect their work and relationships with clients. Clinicians at all levels of experience can benefit from carefully examining what they see, how they think about what they see, and how they eventually act on what they see. To assist counselors in this challenging process, curiosity and creativity become guiding principles. With these principles in mind, clinicians review clinical notes and audio- or videotaped segments searching for clues to enhance self-awareness and clinical service to clients.

☐ Review/Discussion Questions

1. List some practical skills necessary for self-supervision.
2. List some strategies to undertake self-supervision.
3. List and describe the three major focus areas of self-supervision.
4. What is the intended focus of each area?

6
CHAPTER

Self-Supervision and Counselor Self-Care

There is a cost to caring. Professionals who listen to clients' stories of fear, pain, and suffering may feel similar fear, pain, and suffering because they care. Sometimes we feel we are losing our sense of self to the clients we serve.

—Charles R. Figley, 1995

The occupational hazards inherent in the human service professions are beginning to receive increased attention. As documented in the literature, the potential effects on the well-being of helping professionals include stress (e.g., Davies, 1997; Deutsch, 1984; Goldberger & Breznitz, 1993), burnout (e.g., Grosch & Olsen, 1994; Maslach, 1982; Pines, 1993; Warnath, 1979), secondary stress (e.g., Black & Weinreich, 2001; Chrestman, 1995; Cornille & Meyers, 1999; Stamm, 1999), compassion fatigue (e.g., Figley, 1995b), vicarious traumatization (e.g., Pearlman & Saakvitne, 1995; Saakvitne & Pearlman, 1996), critical incident stress (e.g., J. Mitchell, 1994), post-traumatic stress disorder (e.g., American Psychiatric Association, 1994). Kottler and Hazler (1997) encapsulated the work of helping professionals when they remarked, "There are tremendous risks for the therapists in living with the anguish of others, in being so close to others' torments. Sometimes we become desensitized by human emotion and experience an acute overdose of feeling; we turn ourselves off" (p. 7).

Although a seemingly important topic, minimal information regarding work-related issues of counselors is grounded in systematic research; most is based on personal impressions and anecdotal reports (Figley, 1995a;

Norcross & Prochaska, 1986; Thorenson, Miller, & Krauskopf, 1989). As noted by Figley (1995a), most clinical attention is devoted to people in harm's way and "little to those who care for and worry about them" (p. 6). The dearth of systematic research has been attributed to the reluctance of professionals to discuss the discomfort of their work for fear that colleagues will attribute this disclosure to personal inadequacies or professional deficiencies (Warnath, 1979). It has been hypothesized, for example, that counselors who report burnout are shameful that they have failed in the area of their lives of which they are most proud (Grosch & Olsen, 1994). To avoid being perceived as deficient, some professionals retreat, remain self-protective, and internalize emotional distress that can manifest in various ways. This trend takes on particular importance when considering that mental health professionals generally show "significantly higher rates of depression, intense anxiety, and more relationship problems than the general population" (P. White & Franzoni, 1990, p. 258). Based on this finding, it is assumed that negative consequences (e.g., stress, burnout, critical incident stress, compassion fatigue) can result—and directly effect service delivery—when the emotional welfare of counselors is taken for granted or neglected. In other words, counselors are very naïve in thinking that they are immune to the effects of their work.

☐ Forbidden Land

The limited attention rendered to these critical counselor issues appears to reflect a historical trend to neglect work-related problems within the mental health professions (Deutsch, 1984). This trend has been attributed to several factors. Sarason (1977), for example, pointed to the resistance of professional associations to self-scrutiny, society's positive judgment about such work, and fear of professionals demonstrating a human vulnerability. In drawing similar conclusions, Maslach (1982) suggested that (a) burnout is considered antithetical to the professional ideal, (b) professionals are not supposed to experience emotional depletion from their work, and (c) discussion of the demands of the helping profession may dissuade potential recruits.

The inherent difficulty in conducting such sensitive research must also be acknowledged. Concerns surrounding confidentiality and the risk of personal exposure are certainly a worry of counselors and are instrumental in counselors' apprehension of disclosing intimate struggles and dilemmas. Further, taking steps during the self-supervisory process to admit to personal issues that effect treatment can be a daunting task for some professionals. As the focus shifts from clients to self, counselors begin to acknowledge their clinical limitations and human flaws.

☐ Counselor Well-Being and Service Delivery

The importance of addressing counselor emotional well-being is highlighted when we remember that the stability of professionals has direct implications on their service to clients. In further reference, as Sweitzer (1996) noted, "People in the helping professions . . . seem especially vulnerable. The kinds of people who select human services as a career are typically concerned with people and their problems, attuned to human suffering, and anxious to make a difference" (p. 216). Sweitzer's point underscores why it is important for counselors to continually reflect on their professional purpose and emotional status. As human beings, counselors will be affected to varying degrees by events in their own lives. Consequently, it becomes the ethical and professional responsibility of counselors to consider how their personal life events can affect their interactions with clients. Hackney and Cormier (1996) stated, "While no one expects counselors to be perfect, it stands to reason that counselors will be more helpful to clients when they are psychologically intact and not distracted by their own overwhelming problems" (p. 17). They suggested that counselors may be unaware that their own psychological health is marginal, or if they are aware, they continue to provide service and simply use counseling as a defense mechanism to reduce the anxiety they experience about their own issues. Being in a position of power and privilege can provide counselors with a false sense of security. Although they realize that they have personal issues that need to be addressed, they deny the reality of the situation because they consider themselves providers and not recipients of care.

Kottler and Hazler (1997) identified several possible reasons why professionals do not deal with their own problems; they are listed in Table 6.1. Unfortunately, clinicians who deny their own psychological impairment and continue to counsel place clients at risk. Due to their personal problems, counselors become distracted and their judgment is marred. Wiggins Frame and Stevens-Smith (1995) contended that, "Given the

---

TABLE 6.1. Rationalizations of Counselor Avoidance

- I've got to handle this on my own.
- I'll get over it in a little while.
- I can keep it from affecting my work.
- Someone would have told me if it was really a problem.
- It's not as bad as it seems.

From *What You Never Learned in Graduate School* by Jeffrey A. Kottler and Richard J. Hazler. Copyright © 1977 by Jeffrey A. Kotter and Richard J. Hazler. Used by permission of W. W. Norton & Company, Inc.

power of the therapeutic role, impaired counselors who engage in activities that focus on their own needs at the expense of their clients, or are unable to perform their therapeutic responsibilities, may inflict harm on clients" (p. 119).

It is difficult for some people to believe that counselors who have successfully completed the rigors of graduate school training and advanced training can be psychologically impaired. However, research by Norcross and Prochaska (1986) indicated the following:

> Psychotherapists are full of problems we do not expect to find in them. Their problems in living run the entire gamut of human concerns—abortions, affairs, alcoholism, divorce, murder of an old friend, a child's suicide, drug use, a brother on trial for murder—to name just a few described by these psychotherapists. (p. 110)

☐ The Professional and Personal Lives of Counselors

There would be little argument that counseling is a very demanding profession. As noted by Kottler (1991), a counselor's life is fraught with draining days, intense pressures, and personal risks. Nonetheless, the trauma associated with providing counseling has been minimal and the subject is seldom discussed among professionals (e.g., Bentovin, Gorell Barnes, & Cooklin, 1987; Crespi, 1989; Richman, 1986). Luthman and Kirschenbaum (1974) asserted that "it is as though we assume we should be able to handle other people's pain and problems without any cost to ourselves, or at least any admitted cost" (p. 255).

The ways in which counselors can be affected by their work recently hit home during a workshop focusing on the treatment of sex offenders. During a break in the proceedings, a community colleague and I began to chat and exchange comments about the workshop. He was particularly interested in the topic because he worked in a young sex-offender treatment program. While speaking, we got onto the subject of secondary stress and the hazards of working with various client populations, such as sex offenders. As we spoke he began to describe how he felt that his life and schema of the world were changing as a result of his work. He went on to disclose that he was very troubled by the confusion he experienced while he was with his young daughter. More specifically, he was questioning the appropriateness of asking her to sit on his lap or cuddle—behaviors that he had previously found to be natural and spontaneous. To protect his daughter, he found himself avoiding physical contact with her. Because he had joint custody of his daughter, visits were very important to him, yet his thoughts were intruding on their time together. As my colleague shared his story, he expressed a growing confusion about boundaries and the intimacy between parents and children. He candidly and ruefully discussed his distorted view of his relationship with his daughter.

As we were returning to the workshop, I couldn't help but remember a comment by Cerney (1995), who stated that changes in professionals due to their work will be reflected in their interactions with the outside world. These changes, for the most part, are gradual.

☐ Occupational Hazards of Counseling

The personal affects of providing clinical services to clients can be plentiful. Kottler (1991) discussed the occupational hazards of therapeutic practice, including sleepless nights, one-way intimacy, restraint, narcissism, fatigue, futility, isolation, conflict, and money. While discussing how clinicians can absorb the pain of the clients, Figley (1995a) reported that counselors may need assistance in coping with intrusive thoughts, nightmares, and generalized anxiety. In his discussion, Figley introduced the process of *empathic induction*. According to Figley, counselors can be so emotionally aroused by client trauma that they in turn experience emotional upset. He reported that people can become emotionally drained by caring so much that they can be adversely affected by their efforts. In essence, they are traumatized by concern.

Regardless of the impetus underlying client disclosure, what remains significant is that the content of a story, and the process involved in telling the story, can have a tremendous effect on those with whom the story is shared. McCann and Pearlman (1990) elaborate on the constructivist self-development theory (CSDT), which emphasizes integration, meaning, and adaptation. These authors state that CSDT avoids identifying the client as a collection of symptoms and "invites the recognition that each individual is an interactive, complex being striving to survive and to manage a particular set of life circumstances" (p. 56). They suggested that the cognitive schemas of recipients can be disrupted and that the level of disruption to cognitive schemas about self or the world may be subtle or shocking depending on the situation. As proposed by Janoff-Bulmann (1985), three core beliefs that might be challenged in this process include (a) personal vulnerability, (b) the positive view of oneself, and (d) the belief that the world is meaningful and orderly.

In describing an interactional theory of traumatic stress, Wilson (1994) described the level of social, economic, and personal support present as the *trauma membrane*. In this process, significant others tend to form a protective membrane of support around the victim. The secondary stress that can result from participating as part of such a membrane is an emerging concern among counselors. There are advantages and disadvantages of listening to client pain. Advantages can include feeling helpful and an increased level of intimacy or connection. Disadvantages can include feeling overwhelmed and emotionally drained. The distress experienced by caregivers usually pertains to the vicarious trauma coupled with their perceived inability to immediately alleviate the client's pain. In reference to the latter issue, counselors frequently report shutting down emotionally during the disclosure and dialogue process. When explored, this reaction is not propelled by an inherent disinterest, but rather by an automatic self-protective mechanism that serves to guard against further discomfort. This response is similar to what Scott and Stradling (1994) refer to as cognitive avoidance. During this stage, counselors avoid thinking about the traumatic event(s) or aspects of it.

Not knowing how to respond to clients who are disclosing painful information further exasperates the situation, leaving many counselors feeling confused, incompetent, and distraught. Although genuinely interested in alleviating the distress of clients, they are uncertain about how to do so. The feeling of disempowerment can be prompted by stories that evoke concerns about a counselor's own personal power or efficacy in the world (McCann & Pearlman, 1990). Ensuing responses can vary and may include efforts to increase personal safety, heightened awareness regarding the unpredictability of life, increased need for freedom and personal autonomy, and so forth.

As clients vividly describe traumatic events and intentional cruelty, counselors become both witnesses and participants in traumatic reenactments (Pearlman & Saakvitne, 1995). Consequently, they are faced with the challenge of remaining emotionally present and empathic while attempting to ward off vexatious reactions. Herman (1992) suggested that in attempting to gain an understanding of psychological trauma, one comes face to face with human vulnerability and the capacity for evil in human nature. Thus, "when the traumatic events are of human design, those who bear witness are caught in the conflict between victim and perpetrator" (Herman, 1992, p. 7).

Although not all counselors experience trauma, the potential influence of a story on counselors warrants attention. As stated earlier, the vicarious trauma experienced by an individual can extend beyond the self and have ramifications for immediate family, friends, and colleagues. The complex interconnectedness of clients and counselors was emphasized by Remer and Ferguson (1995) who wrote:

> Therapeutic intervention is necessary to support the healing of the primary victim while at the same time supporting that of the secondary victims and to find a balance between the requirements of the primary victim healing and the requirements of the secondary victim. (p. 411)

The individual who experiences secondary stress may experience a sense of disorientation, terror, and vulnerability. Not realizing the extent to which they have been influenced as a result of listening to a painful narrative, counselors may initially have difficulty accounting for mood and behavioral vacillations. Because the described event did not directly involve them, many helping professionals struggle to associate their emotional disposition with the narrative that unfolded in front of them.

☐ Existing Constructs

There are a number of major constructs pertaining to the occupational hazards of counseling. Although they share common ground, there are differences that counselors might find important when assessing their own physical, emotional, behavioral, and spiritual well-being during self-supervision. The following descriptions are merely overviews to acquaint readers with the various ways in which counselors may be affected by their work.

Burnout

Burnout has been reviewed extensively in the literature (e.g., Farber, 1983; Freudenberger, 1974; Grosch & Olsen, 1994; Pines, 1993; Schaufeli, Maslach, & Marek, 1993). Pines pointed out that burnout was introduced to the scientific literature in the early 1970s by Freudenberger and Maslach. To assist professionals in assessing their circumstances, several inventories are also available, including the Maslach Burnout Inventory (Maslach and Jackson, 1981), the Burnout Measure (Pines & Aronson, 1988), and the Psychologist Burnout Inventory (Ackerly, Burnell, Holder, & Kurdel, 1988).

Burnout has been defined as a state of extreme dissatisfaction with one's work, is characterized by (a) excessive distancing from clients, (b) impaired competence, (c) low energy, (d) increased irritability with supporters, and (e) other signs of impairment and depression resulting from individual, social and work environment, and (f) social factors (Figley, 1995a). Pines and Aronson (1988) defined burnout as "a state of physical, emotional and mental exhaustion caused by long term involvement in emotionally demanding situations" (p. 9). Kottler and Hazler (1997) proposed that burnout may be better described as *rustout:* "a degenerative process where a variety of symptoms emerge" (p. 193). This latter point was emphasized by Grosch and Olsen (1994), who stated that burnout was not just tiredness, but rather an erosion of spirit. These authors expressed that, "It is important to realize that burnout is not just a condition

---

TABLE 6.2. Burnout

---

1. Burnout is a process, not a fixed condition, that begins gradually and becomes progressively worse.
2. The process includes (a) gradual exposure to job strain, (b) erosion of idealism, and (c) a void of achievement.
3. There is an accumulation of intensive contact with clients.

Adapted from Figley, copyright 1995 in *Compassion Fatigue: Coping with secondary traumatic stress.* Reprinted with permission of Brunner-Routledge, a member of the Taylor & Francis Group.

of the body, but also of the soul. It involves a loss of faith in the very enterprise of helping" (p. 4).

Figley (1995a) asserted that burnout was cumulative, relatively predictable, and associated with multiple sources of stress. He further stated that burnout was a collection of symptoms associated with emotional exhaustion and provided a very useful description as outlined in Table 6.2.

During the self-supervision process, when reviewing their emotional, physical, and spiritual status, counselors can review symptoms of burnout that have been consolidated by Figley (1995a) and Grosch and Olsen (1994) as illustrated in Table 6.3. Grosch and Olsen suggested that professionals often do not recognize the problem of burnout until it has reached an advanced stage. In their opinion, the early stages of burnout are typically attributed to simple tiredness, low energy, or boredom.

Warnath and Shelton (1976) pointed to the discrepancy between graduate school idealism and on-the-job reality as a leading factor in counselor burnout. Based on their personal experience, Warnath and Shelton highlighted differences between young (1 to 4 years of experience) counselors and those with 10 or more years of experience. According to these authors, novice counselors are often caught off guard by their increased counseling work load, a perceived lack of client appreciation, and pressure to become more efficient in their work.

Pines (1993) wrote, "Individuals who enter a profession (e.g., nursing or counseling) with a cynical attitude are unlikely to burn out; but those with a strong desire to give of themselves and who feel helpful, excited, and idealistic are susceptible to the most severe burnout" (p. 386). She further noted that people cannot burn out unless they were *on fire* to begin with.

Stress

Stress has also received enormous attention and has been defined in a number of ways throughout the literature (Breznitz & Goldberger, 1993).

TABLE 6.3. Symptoms of Burnout

1. Physical symptoms: fatigue and physical depletion or exhaustion; sleep difficulties; specific somatic problems such as headaches, gastrointestinal disturbances, back pain, weight loss, colds, and flu.
2. Emotional symptoms: irritability, emptiness, anxiety, depression, guilt, sense of helplessness, negative self-concept, guilt, self-blame for not accomplishing more with clients.
3. Behavioral symptoms: aggression, callousness, pessimism, defensiveness, cynicism, substance abuse, loss of enthusiasm, quickness to frustration and anger, boredom, becoming increasingly rigid, difficulty making decisions.
4. Work-related symptoms: quitting the job, poor work performance, arriving at work late, working long hours but accomplishing little, absenteeism, tardiness, misuse of work breaks, thefts.
5. Interpersonal symptoms: perfunctory communication with, inability to concentrate/focus on, and/or withdrawal from clients and/or coworkers; and then dehumanizing and intellectualizing clients.
6. Spiritual symptoms: loss of faith, meaning, and purpose; crisis of values, heightened scrupulosity or changes in religious ideas and affiliations.

Adapted from Figley, copyright 1995 in *Compassion Fatigue: Coping with secondary traumatic stress.* Reprinted with permission of Brunner-Routledge, a member of the Taylor & Francis Group.
Adapted from *When Helping Starts to Hurt: A new look at burnout among psychotherapists* by William N. Grosch and David C. Olsen. Copyright © 1994 by William N. Grosch and David C. Olsen. Used by permission of W. W. Norton & Company, Inc.

In providing a working definition, Stoyva and Carlson (1993) suggested that psychological stress "refers to a situation in which the challenges or threats facing the individual exceed his or her estimated coping mechanisms" (p. 729). According to Pines (1993), "Stress happens to more people and in more situations than burnout" (p. 386). It was her contention that stress did not cause burnout and that people are able to excel in stressful situations if they feel that their work is meaningful. There are several scales that are designed to assess stressful life events. Examples include the Stress Appraisal Measurement (Peacock & Wong, 1990), the Social Readjustment Rating Scale (Holmes & Rahe, 1967), the Hassles Scale (Kanner, Coyne, Schaefer, & Lazarus, 1981), the Questionnaire on Resources and Stress (Holroyd, 1988), and the Psychiatric Epidemiological Research Interview-Life Events Scale (Dohrenwend & Dohrenwend, 1978). Gibson and Mitchell (1999) have outlined several work-related factors that may result in counselor stress, as described in Table 6.4.

In terms of stress that can emerge when working with clients, Harris and Maloney (1996) have consolidated the work of several authors regarding client behaviors that might cause counselors stress. These behav-

---

TABLE 6.4. Factors Contributing to Counselor Stress

- Too many demanding, frustrating, or otherwise stressful situations
- Constant pressure to do more than can be done
- Too much time-consuming yet unrewarding work (e.g., paperwork)
- Constant conflicts between competing alternatives for time and effort (e.g., home and work)
- Persistent demands for skills or knowledge that appear to be beyond that possessed by the individual
- Constant interference or interruptions of planned or anticipated activities
- Lack of clarity or direction regarding work expectancies
- Lack of positive feedback, recognition, reward, or notice of efforts or accomplishments
- Depressing work environment
- Poor interpersonal relationships
- Constant disillusions or disappointments
- All work and no play, failure to lead a balanced lifestyle

Gibson and Mitchell, copyright 1999 in *Counseling and Guidance*. Reprinted with permission of Pearson Education, Inc.

iors are summarized in Table 6.5. Corey, Corey, and Callanan (1993) suggested that counselors should remain aware of personal values that underpin their work. When there is a clash between client and counselor values (e.g., difference of value placed on personal agency), a counselor might find client responses or behaviors stressful.

TABLE 6.5. Stressful Client Behaviors

- Clients who "play the game": they go along with agency rules but they're not really making progress.
- Clients who lie to you.
- Clients who manipulate you to get something they want but cannot have.
- Clients who are never satisfied with what you have to give; they always seem to need more.
- Clients who are prone to angry outbursts at you.
- Clients who blame everyone but themselves for their problems.
- Clients who are always negative about everything.
- Clients who are sullen and give one-word answers or responses.
- Clients who ask again and again for suggestions and then reject every one.
- Clients who refuse to see their behavior as a problem.
- Clients who are very passive and won't do anything to help themselves.

Taken from Harris and Maloney (1996). Reprinted with permission of Allyn and Bacon, Boston, MA.

Critical Incident Stress

A critical incident has been defined by the International Critical Incident Stress Foundation (ICISF, 2000) as "any event that is outside the normal range of human emotion and has the potential to pierce our emotional armour." As a result of the emotional trauma associated with significant critical events, normal coping mechanisms break down. This response can dramatically affect how professionals function at work, with their families, and socially.

According to J. Mitchell (1994), critical incident stress (CIS) stems from a single event or a series of very traumatic events that overwhelm the professional's resources. Some of the significant events reported by helping professionals include death of children, injury to children, death of any person, threatening events, knowing the victim, and grotesque sights and sounds exhibited by victims. To better articulate CIS, the ICISF identified *critical incident stress syndrome* as a milder reaction to a stressor and *critical incident stress disorder* as a severe reaction to a stress stimuli.

The ICISF has provided an extensive list of signs and symptoms of CIS. The list is divided into physical (e.g., chills, thirst, nausea, dizziness), cognitive (e.g., confusion, nightmares, uncertainty, hypervigilance), emotional (e.g., fear, guilt, grief, panic), and behavioral (e.g., withdrawal, antisocial acts, inability to rest, intensified pacing) indicators. In addition, the ICISF has provided several suggestions for affected individuals and their families and elaborate CIS debriefing procedures.

Traumatic Stress

Volpe (2000) stated that, "Traumatic stress encompasses exposure to events or the witnessing of events that are extreme and/or life threatening." He further noted that traumatic events are usually unexpected and uncontrollable. As such, such events may lead individuals to question their safety and security, thus leaving them feeling vulnerable and insecure.

Traumatic events can be distinguished as Type I and Type II. Type I events are considered short term and can include natural (e.g., hurricanes, floods) and accidental (motor vehicle accidents, fires) disasters as well as deliberate disasters caused by people (e.g., rape, assault and battery). These events are abrupt and generally last for a few minutes or as long as a few hours.

Type II traumatic events are generally sustained and repeated over a period of time. These events involve chronic, repeated, and ongoing exposure (Volpe, 2000). Natural and technological disasters can include chronic illness and toxic spills. It was suggested that events resulting from intentional human acts include child sexual abuse and spousal abuse. It is important to remain mindful of the implications associated with serving clients who have been traumatized. Volpe elaborated

> It is important to consider that research indicates that, despite the hetero- geneity of traumatic events, individuals who directly or vicariously experi- ence such events show similar profiles of psychopathology including chronic PTSD and commonly observed comorbid disorders such as depression, gen- eralized anxiety disorder, and substance abuse.

Compassion Fatigue

The study of traumatic stress has primarily been associated with post- traumatic stress disorder (American Psychiatric Association, 1994; M. Williams & Sommer, 1994). Thus, clinical attention has surged toward individuals directly afflicted by a shocking event. Unfortunately, during this process, the emotional needs of individuals closely related to victims have been overlooked. In addressing the cumulative effect of client prob- lems on counselors, Pearlman and Saakvitne (1995) asserted that coun- selors are asked to remain hopeful in the face of overwhelming despair. They wrote:

> We are asked to witness brutal behavior to someone we not only care about but also to whom we have made a commitment to help. We are asked to understand feelings that are abhorrent to us: self-hatred, the wish to die or to destroy one's body, vicious misogyny, and complete nihilism. In the face of these feelings, we are left holding the wish for our client's life, health, and happiness. (p. 92)

Compassion fatigue has been defined as a state of tension and preoccu- pation with individual or cumulative trauma of clients as manifested in one or more ways, including (a) reexperiencing the traumatic event, (b) avoidance or numbing of reminders of the event, and (c) persistent arousal. Compassion fatigue is identical to secondary traumatic stress and has to do with the nature of helping professional work. This emotional state can emerge suddenly, without much warning, and carries with it a sense of helplessness, confusion, and isolation. Professionals working with suffer- ing clients must contend with both the normal stress and dissatisfaction of work and also their emotional and personal feelings for distressed cli- ents. Perhaps more stressful and possibly detrimental to a counselor's mental health is that, "empathizing with and being devoted to victims opens the helper to feeling all the maladaptive stressors and traumatic responses of victims. Hence the initially adaptive identification and un- derstanding of victims may lapse into the helper's becoming a fellow vic-

---

TABLE 6.6. Symptoms of Counselor Psychological Distress

---

1. Distressing emotions: sadness or grief, depression, anxiety, dread and horror, fear, rage, or shame.
2. Intrusive imagery by the trauma worker of the client's traumatic material: nightmares, flooding, and flashbacks of images generated during and following the client's recounting of traumatic events.
3. Numbing or avoidance of efforts to elicit or work with traumatic material from the client, including disassociation.
4. Somatic complaints: sleep difficulty, headaches, gastrointestinal distress, and heart palpitations.
5. Addictive or compulsive behaviors: substance abuse, workaholism, and compulsive eating.
6. Physiological arousal.
7. Impairment of day-to-day functioning in social and personal roles, such as missed or cancelled appointments; decreased use of supervision or co-therapy; chronic lateness; a decreased ability to engage in self-care behaviors, including personal therapy; feelings of isolation, alienation, or lack of appreciation.

Taken from Dutton and Rubinstein (1995). Reprinted with permission by Taylor & Francis.

tim" (Valent, 1995, p. 45). As researchers have become more cognizant of helper trauma, they have begun to investigate the area of secondary traumatization, now referred to as compassion fatigue (Figley, 1995a). A self-test for psychotherapists designed to measure compassion fatigue has been constructed by Figley (1995a).

Dutton and Rubinstein (1995) noted that there was an array of secondary stress reactions that counselors could experience as a result of working with traumatized clients. Included were psychological distress or dysfunction, changes in cognitive schema, and relational disturbances. Indicators of psychological distress or dysfunction are outlined in Table 6.6.

In terms of counselor cognitions, there may be a shift in beliefs, expectations, and assumptions. Dutton and Rubenstein (1995) also discussed *witness guilt* or *clinician guilt* whereby counselors may "feel guilty for enjoying life when she or he sees the struggle of a survivor" (p. 86). Secondary exposure to trauma may also affect counselors' personal and professional relationships. Moreover, they can struggle with trust and intimacy after listening to client narratives.

Finally, counselors may become increasingly distant from clients, colleagues, and family. Professionals may exhibit distancing behaviors toward clients by judging, labeling, or pathologizing their reactions; dissociating during interviews; or being chronically late for appointments. With colleagues or family members, counselors may withdraw, become isolated, and think that their distress reaction could not be understood by others.

Vicarious Traumatization

Pearlman and Saakvitne (1995) asserted that the effects of vicarious traumatization were widespread, and its costs immeasurable. In their opinion, the experience of vicarious traumatization inevitably affects professional and personal relationships. They defined vicarious traumatization as "the transformation in the inner experience of the therapist that comes about as a result of the empathic engagement with clients' trauma material" (p. 31). According to Pearlman and Saakvitne, this material can include graphic descriptions of violent events, exposure to the realities of people's cruelty to one another, and involvement in or witnessing traumatic events.

Due to the central role counselors can play in the lives of clients, it is inevitable that they will be privy to a myriad of emotional problems experienced by clients. Consequently, these professionals are at risk of absorbing the emotional pain of their clients. Pearlman and MacIan (1995) elaborated:

> Vicarious traumatization implies changes in the therapist's enduring ways of experiencing self, others, and the world. The effects of vicarious trauma-

---

TABLE 6.7. Effects of Traumatic Events

- **General frame of reference**
  Personal identity: Disconnection from one's usual experience of oneself
  World view: A disruption to one's perception of the world, people, and life philosophy
  Spirituality: A disruption to one's spiritual base
- **Self capacities**
  Self-Soothing: Inability to maintain a positive self-esteem and to self-sooth
- **Ego resources**
  Cognitive processing: Inability to make self-protective judgments, become introspective, maintain boundaries
- **Psychological needs**
  Safety: An increased sense of fearfulness, vulnerability to harm, increased fears about significant others
  Trust: A lack of trust in oneself and a growing dependence on others to meet personal needs
  Esteem: Development of self-criticism, self-harm behaviors
  Intimacy: A lack of self-intimacy and intimacy with others
  Control: Increased sense of helplessness and decreased sense of control
- **Sensory system**
  Imagery: Imposing and distressing images that intrude on a counselor's life
  Bodily experiences: Bodily experiences that parallel those described by clients
  Other sensory experiences: Sounds, smells

Taken from Pearlman, L. and Saakvitne, K. (1995). Reprinted with permission from *Trauma and the Therapist: Countertransference and vicarious traumatization in psychotherapy with incest survivors*. New York: Norton.

tization permeate the therapist's inner world and relationships. These effects do not arise solely from one therapy relationship; we posit that they are cumulative across time and helping relationships. (p. 558)

Pearlman and MacIan (1995) elaborated on how various aspects of a counselor's life could be affected as a result of listening to or witnessing traumatic events; these effects are summarized in Table 6.7.

Of the five existing constructs describing the work-related experiences of counselors, only stress and critical incident stress have been empirically investigated. When considering the available information, much of what has been reported about counselor well-being has been based on personal experiences, general observations, and is limited by a lack of empirical evidence.

☐ Proactive Strategies for Counselors

It is not a question of whether counselors' well-being will be affected by their demanding work, but rather, to what degree. To move beyond the problem identification stage (emotional distress of counselors), it is necessary to create practical strategies designed to assist counselors in avoiding, managing, or resolving their emotional turmoil. As such, several proactive steps for counselors are suggested below.

Anticipating Emotional Distress

Realizing that they will be facing increased demands and interacting with clients who will be presenting with a variety of mental health problems, it is important that counselors prepare themselves accordingly. Counselors need to understand that being emotionally affected by client problems is normal and is not indicative of personal deficiencies. Pearlman and McCann (1995), for example, noted that vicarious traumatization reflects neither pathology in counselors nor intentionality on the part of clients.

As discussed earlier, however, there may be situations when counselors will need to seek consultation or professional assistance in order to resolve personal issues that are triggered by specific client concerns or behaviors. In general, how counselors deal with their emotional pain is a critical question. An advantage of anticipating emotional distress is that counselors can normalize their reactions when they emerge and better appreciate the demands of their work.

The anticipation of severe client problems may be particularly helpful for beginning counselors or counselors who are moving from one geographical area to another. Consulting with colleagues may be the most effective and efficient way to learn about a different client population and prevalent presenting problems (e.g., increased drug use, domestic violence, child abuse or neglect). Having an idea of what to expect can better acclimatize counselors, reduce the element of surprise, and lessen the impact of client issues.

Maintaining Personal Awareness

Despite counselors' vulnerability, there are distinct signs that they themselves, colleagues, and significant others can notice that indicate counselor despair. Although some signs are subtle and not easily detected, typical examples suggesting counselor distress include withdrawal, persistent sadness, reduced energy, and emotional overinvolvement.

The ability to personally recognize signs of emotional distress, however, can be particularly elusive for professionals who are immersed in the helping process. Rather than focusing on one's own personal wellbeing, counselors can easily neglect their own needs while attending to the needs of clients. The propensity to neglect personal needs may be a common response since the majority of attention has been directed toward clients and minimal attention has been devoted to professionals who care for and worry about them (Figley, 1995a). Remaining vigilant about the rigors of counseling and the potential impact this work can have on professionals can prompt counselor sensitivity to secondary traumatization and the need for personal well-being. To maintain a sense of balance and professional well-being, Yassen (1995) emphasized the importance of personal nutrition, exercise, sleep, relaxation, and creative expression.

Identifying Client Populations

There may be a specific client population(s) or a presenting problem(s) that will contribute to counselors' emotional despair more than others. For example, one school counselor realized that young children who appeared disheveled and neglected contributed to a sense of helplessness and prolonged sadness. His personal disposition became problematic when he found himself unable to function normally with other students following interactions with students who appeared unstable and vulnerable. Counselors who attempt to work with challenging client populations may experience a sudden loss of counseling maneuverability due to their own emotional turmoil. Professionals who are emotionally affected by a specific client problem(s) may find that their ability to intervene objectively is thwarted. Rather than considering client needs, and corresponding goals and strategies, these counselors experience a sense of uncertainty and excessive concern. After identifying specific client populations that may be personally troublesome, counselors can seek additional support and consultation to ensure adequate care and personal well-being. In larger centers, where there may be more than one counselor, the benefit of referring clients to a colleague may exist. The intention of the referral process is not to promote counselor avoidance of highly charged personal issues, but rather to ensure adequate client care.

Developing a Plan of Action

Knowing that they will experience situations that will affect them emotionally, counselors can be pro-active and design specific strategies to maintain a sense of balance and well-being. Typical strategies are described below and include maintaining a support network, maintaining membership in a professional organization, attending organizational meetings, maintaining realistic goals, exercising and taking vacation time, and seeking mental health consultation for personal issues.

Maintaining a Support Network

Counselors can develop a social support network consisting of colleagues, friends, and family. As stated earlier, counselors are not always able to detect emotional and behavioral changes within themselves and need to rely on others for an outsider perspective. In maintaining a social support network it becomes the responsibility of counselors to inform colleagues and significant others about the inherent challenges of their work, and more importantly, their vulnerability. Being able to share personal experiences while respecting issues of confidentiality provides counselors with opportunities to openly express themselves while receiving valuable feedback and support. By doing so, counselors can reduce the propensity toward personal and professional isolation and the harmful effects associated with ruminating about work-related issues. In discussing occupational stress within the counseling profession, Sowa, May, and Niles (1994) contended that, "Professional support and supervision groups, as well as the use of professional mentors, may need to be established within the context of counselors' occupational settings to provide the resources of social support" (p. 27).

In emphasizing the need to create a support system, Yager and Park (1986) encouraged counselors to meet with other counselors who are working in similar jobs. These authors noted that by sharing difficulties with colleagues, counselors might be able to reformulate problems and discover insights that might not occur in isolation.

Participating in Organizational Membership and Meetings

Participation in professional organizations and meetings can assist counselors in remaining connected with colleagues and abreast of new developments in the field. A bonus to a membership is the accompanying journal and/or newsletter. Sometimes, it is not what is said during a conference workshop that is most helpful. For many, it is informal hallway chats that counselors enjoy. While sharing stories with colleagues, counselors are confirmed and the challenges of their work are validated. During these chats, old relationships are rekindled and new relationships are established. Informal conversations can serve to normalize feelings of sadness, frustration, and so forth.

Establishing Realistic Goals

Yager and Park (1986) suggested that counselors ask themselves a basic question: What is the focus of my functioning as a counselor? Although seemingly simplistic, its importance cannot be overemphasized. This question invites counselors to review its purpose, goals, and results. Yager and Park contended that, "Too often counselors, in an attempt to *remain current* [italics in original] gain new professional information in a haphazard, indiscriminate fashion. As a result, they invest their energy in acquiring skills only remotely related to those necessary for current professional needs." Establishing realistic goals, and articulating steps to achieve such goals can help counselors experience incremental successes. Grandiose clinical treatment plans are fine in theory, but in reality are rarely achieved. Rather than creating manageable objectives, well-intended counselors become overenthusiastic and place pressure on themselves and clients to reach nonrealistic goals.

Seeking Mental Health Consultation

Despite the historical trend of professional and personal avoidance of self-scrutinizing, counselors need to understand the importance of maintaining a personal sense of well-being. When personal issues are triggered by their work, counselors are encouraged to seek appropriate help in order to process what they are experiencing. Assuming that personal issues will simply vanish or will not effect their work heightens counselor and client vulnerability.

Counselor education programs can be instrumental in preparing aspiring professionals for the rigors of the counseling profession. Sowa, May, and Niles (1994) elaborated: "Just as counselors seek to empower their clients in determining physical and psychological health, counselor educators may need to provide their students with opportunities to develop important resources in coping with the stress of being counselors" (p. 28). Sowa, May, and Niles (1994) recommended stress management courses that underscore coping-skills training in counselor education programs. To support this recommendation, it is important that a safe, confidential, and respectful atmosphere be established wherein counselors can candidly discuss their daily challenges and concerns.

☐ Conclusion

As the counseling landscape evolves and the job requirements continue to change for counselors, it is imperative that their emotional well-being be carefully considered. As discussed in this chapter, helping professionals are generally reluctant to disclose personal distress, and as a result may retreat into professional isolation. Major concerns associated with this decision are counselor personal well-being and his or her ability to adequately assist clients.

To augment the literature on existing constructs regarding the occupational hazards associated with counseling, this chapter outlined several practical steps counselors can consider to maintain a sense of balance and well-being. It should be underscored that the suggested strategies are not empirically based and therefore should be viewed sagaciously.

☐ Review/Discussion Questions

1. Why is counselor well-being important?
2. List and describe some occupational hazards associated with counseling.
3. List and describe some proactive strategies that counselors can use to promote personal well-being.

EPILOGUE

From the outset, my intention in writing this book was straightforward: to contribute to the counselor and helping professional development literature. It is my hope that a spin-off of this work will eventuate in enhanced counselor well-being and improved clinical service.

Although self-supervision is not a new idea, I believe that this unique practice warrants closer examination in order to determine its value. Over the years, several authors (some more than others) have brushed against the idea of counselor self-monitoring. Perhaps, as this practice is reconsidered, new inroads will be made

A gifted colleague, Dr. James Nowlin, who oversees the School Counselor Education Program at Montana State University-Billings, continually encourages people to create *ideas that others can rub against*. He promotes differences of opinions and, most of all, welcomes creativity and innovation. As I was writing this book, I often thought about James and his invitation. I hope that I was successful in providing such ideas.

Clearly, not everyone will endorse or embrace the self-supervision process. Still, there will be practitioners who will support this practice to varying degrees. Such a divergence of opinions should be celebrated and encouraged! It is precisely this divergence that makes the helping professions exciting and vibrant. I shy away from the *one size fits all approach* and invite readers to determine what, if any, aspect of self-supervision is personally useful. Self-supervision is not a true and proven process, but rather, one that counselors can mull over and experiment with. I realize that this book will not meet the needs of all its readers. Some will want more information in one area while others will want information in another area. I hope that these gaps will be closed in the future.

Finally, the most exciting aspect of publishing this book, for me, is the anticipation of productive criticism from readers, future research, and the refinement of the self-supervision practice. I look forward to reading about or hearing the different reactions from colleagues.

REFERENCES

Ackerly, G., Burnell, J., Holder, D., & Kurdek, L. (1988). Burnout among licensed psychologists. *Professional Psychology: Research and Practice, 19,* 624–631.

Allman, L. (1982). The aesthetic preference: Overcoming the pragmatic error. *Family Process, 21,* 43–56.

Altekruse, M., & Brown, D. (1969). Counselor behavior change through self-analysis. *Counselor Education and Supervision, 8,* 108–122.

American Psychiatric Association. (1994). *Diagnostic and statistical manual of mental disorders* (4th ed.). Washington, DC: Author.

Amundson, J., Stewart, K., & Valentine, L. (1993). Temptations of power and certainty. *Journal of Marital and Family Therapy, 19,* 111–132.

Anderson, C., & Stewart, S. (1983). *Mastering resistance: A practical guide to family therapy.* New York: Guilford.

Anderson, S., Schlossberg, M., & Rigazio-DiGilio, S. (2000). Family therapy trainees' evaluations of their best and worst supervision experiences. *Journal of Marital and Family Therapy, 26,* 79–91.

Andersen, T. (1987). The reflecting team: Dialogue and meta-dialogue in clinical work. *Family Process, 26,* 415–428.

Andersen, T. (1991). *The reflecting team: Dialogues and dialogues about dialogues.* New York: Norton

Aponte, H. (1992). Training the person-of-the-therapist in structural family therapy. *Journal of Marital and Family Therapy, 18,* 269–281.

Aponte, H. (1994a). *Bread and spirit: Therapy with the new poor.* New York: Norton.

Aponte, H. (1994b). How personal can training get? *Journal of Marital and Family Therapy, 20,* 1–15.

Aponte, H., & Winter, J. (1987). The person and practice of the therapist: Treatment and training. In M. Baldwin & V. Satir (Eds.), *The use of self in therapy* (pp. 84-111). New York: Haworth.

Argyris, C. (1976). Theories of action that inhibit individual learning. *American Psychologist, 31,* 638–654.

Argyris, C., Putnam, R., & Smith, D. (1987). *Action science: Concepts, methods and skills for research and intervention.* San Francisco: Jossey-Bass.

Arnold, E., & Boggs, K. (1995). *Interpersonal relationships: Professional communication skills for nurses* (2nd ed.). Philadelphia: Saunders.

Arthur, H. (1995). Student self-evaluations: How useful? How valid? *International Journal of Nursing Studies, 32,* 271–276.

Atkinson, B., & Lehmann, P. (1984). Study of compassion fatigue. *The Bond, 18,* 2.

Baker, C. (1996). Reflective learning: A teaching strategy for critical thinking. *Journal of Nursing Education, 35,* 19–22.

Baldwin, M. (1987). Interview with Carl Rogers on the use of the self in therapy. In M. Baldwin & V. Satir (Eds.), *The use of self in therapy* (pp. 45–52). New York: Haworth.

Bandura, A. (1978). The self system in reciprocal determinism. *American Psychologist, 33,* 344–358.

Baruth, L., & Manning, M. (1999). *Multicultural counseling and psychotherapy* (2nd ed.). Upper Saddle River, NJ: Prentice Hall.

Bentovin, A., Gorell Barnes, G., & Cooklin, A. (Eds.). (1987). *Family therapy: Complementary frameworks of theory and practice.* London: Academic Press.

Bernard, J., & Goodyear, R. (1992). *Fundamentals of clinical supervision.* Boston: Allyn & Bacon.

Bernard, J., & Goodyear, R. (1998). *Fundamentals of clinical supervision* (2nd ed.). Boston: Allyn & Bacon.

Bernstein, B., & Lecomte, C. (1979). Self-critique technique training in a competency-based practicum. *Counselor Education and Supervision, 19,* 69–76.

Black, S., & Weinreich, P. (2001). An exploration of counseling identity in counselors who deal with trauma [Electonic version]. *Traumatology, 6,* 1.

Blum, H. (1995). The Irma dream, self-analysis, and self-supervision. *Journal of the American Psychoanalysis Association, 44,* 511–531.

Boyd, E., & Fales, A. (1983). Reflective learning: Key to learning from experience. *Journal of Human Psychology, 23,* 99–117.

Bradley, L. (1989). *Counselor supervision: Principles, process, and practice.* Muncie, IN: Accelerated Development.

Bradmiller, L. (1978). Self-disclosure in the helping relationship. *Social Work, 14,* 28–35.

Braverman, S. (1984). Family of origin as a training resource for family therapists. In C. Munson (Ed.), *Family of origin applications in clinical supervision* (pp. 37–47). New York: Haworth.

Breznitz, S., & Goldberger, L. (1993). Stress research at a crossroads. In L. Goldberger & S. Breznitz (Eds.), *Handbook of stress: Theoretical and clinical aspects* (2nd ed.). New York: Free Press.

Brookfield, S. (1987). *Developing critical thinkers.* San Francisco: Jossey-Bass.

Bross, A. (1982). *Strategic family therapy.* Toronto, ON: Metheun.

Bruelin, D., Karper, B., McGuire, D., & Cimmarusti, R. (1988). Cybernetics of videotape supervision. In H. Liddle, D. Breulin, & R. Schwartz (Eds.), *Handbook of family therapy training and supervision* (pp. 194–206). New York: Guilford.

Butler, M., & Bird, M. (2000). Narrative and interactional process for preventing harmful struggle in therapy: An integrative empirical mode. *Journal of Marital and Family Therapy, 26,* 123–142.

Cade, B., & Cornwell, M. (1985). New realities for old: Some uses of teams and one way screens in therapy. In D. Campbell & R. Draper (Eds.), *Applications of systemic family therapy: The Milan approach* (pp. 47–57). London: Grune & Stratton.

Campbell, D., Draper, R., & Huffington, C. (1991). *Second thoughts on the theory and practice of the Milan approach to family therapy.* New York: Karnac Books.

Casey, P., Smith, K., & Ulrich, S. (1989). *Self-supervision: A career tool for audiologist and speech-language pathologist.* Rockville, MD: National Student Speech and Hearing Association.

Cecchin, G., Lane, G., & Ray, W. (1992). *Irreverence: A strategy for therapists' survival.* New York: Karnac Books.

Cecchin, G., Lane, G., & Ray, W. (1993). From strategizing to nonintervention: Toward irreverence in systemic practice. *Journal of Marital and Family Therapy, 19,* 125–136.

Cerney, M. (1995). Treating the "heroic treaters." In C. Figley (Ed.), *Compassion fatigue: Coping with secondary traumatic stress disorder in those who treat the traumatized* (pp. 131–149). New York: Brunner/Mazel

Chenail, R. (1997). Interviewing exercises: Lessons from family therapy. *The Qualitative Report, 3,* #2 [Electronic version]

Collins, P. (1993). The interpersonal vicissitudes of mentorship: An exploratory study of the field supervisor-student relationship. *The Clinical Supervisor, 11,* 121–135.

Copeland, W., Birmingham, C., De La Cruz, E., & Lewin, B. (1993). The reflective practitioner in teaching: Toward a research agenda. *Teaching and Teacher Education, 9,* 347–359.

Corey, G. (1997). *Theory and practice of counseling and psychotherapy* (5th ed.). Pacific Grove, CA: Brooks Cole.

Corey, G., Corey, M., & Callanan, P. (1993). *Issues and ethics in the helping professions* (4th ed.) Pacific Grove, CA: Brooks/Cole.

Cormier, L., & Cormier, W. (1976). Developing and implementing self-instructional modules for counselor training. *Counselor Education and Supervision, 16,* 37–45.

Cornille, T., & Meyers, T. (1999). Secondary traumatic stress among child protective service workers: Prevalence, severity, and predictive factors. *Traumatology, 5, 1.*

Cornwell, M., & Pearson, R. (1981). Cotherapy teams and one-way screens in family therapy practice and training. *Family Process, 20,* 199–209.

Coyne, J., Wortman, C., & Lehman, D. (1988). The other side of support: Emotional overinvolvement and miscarried helping. In B. H. Gottlieb (Ed.), *Marshalling social support* (pp. 305–330). Thousand Oaks, CA: Sage.

Crago, M. (1987). Supervision and self-exploration. In M. Crago & M. Pickering (Eds.), *Supervision in human communication disorders* (pp. 137–158). Boston: College-Brown.

Crespi, T. (1989). *Child and adolescent psychopathology and involuntary hospitalization: A handbook for mental health professionals.* Springfield, IL: Charles C. Thomas.

Davies, R. (Ed.). (1997). *Stress in social work.* London: Jessica Kingsley Publishers.

deShazer, S. (1982). Some conceptual distinctions are more useful than others. *Family Process, 21,* 71–84.

deShazer, S. (1985). *Keys to solutions in brief therapy.* New York: Norton.

deShazer, S. (1994). *Words were originally magic.* New York: Norton.

Deutsch, C. (1984). Self-reported sources of stress among psychotherapists. *Professional Psychology: Research Theory and Practice, 15,* 833–845.

Devore, W., & Schlesinger, E. (1999). *Ethnic-sensitive social work practice* (5th ed.). Needham Heights, MA: Allyn and Bacon.

Dewey, J. (1933). *How we think.* Chicago: Regnery.

DiBlasio, P., Fischer, J., & Prata, G. (1986). The telephone chart: A cornerstone of the first interview with the family. *Journal of Strategic and Systemic Therapies, 5,* 31–44.

Dohrenwend, B., & Dohrenwend, B. (1978). Some issues in research on stressful life events. *Journal of Mental and Nervous Disorders, 153,* 207–234.

Donnelly, C., & Glaser, A. (1992). Training in self-supervision skills. *The Clinical Supervisor, 10,* 85-96.

Dowling, S. (1979). Developing student self-supervisory skills in clinical training. *Journal of the National Student Speech and Hearing Association, 7,* 37–41.

Dutton, M., & Rubenstein, F. (1995). Working with people with PTSD: Research implications. In C. Figley (Ed.), *Compassion fatigue: Coping with secondary traumatic stress disorder in those who treat the traumatized* (pp. 82–100). New York: Brunner/Mazel.

Edelwich, J., & Brodsky, A. (1991). *Sexual dilemmas for the helping professional.* New York: Brunner/Mazel.

Efran, J., Lukens, M., & Lukens, R. (1990). *Language, structure and change: Frameworks of meaning in psychotherapy.* New York: Norton.

Eraut, M. (1995). Schon shock: A case for reframing reflection in action. *Teachers and Teaching, 1*(1), 9–22.

Farber, B. (1983). *Stress and burn-out in the human service professions.* New York: Pergamon.

Figley, C. (1995a). Compassion fatigue as secondary traumatic stress disorder: An overview. In C. Figley (Ed.), *Compassion fatigue: Coping with secondary traumatic stress disorder in those who treat the traumatized* (pp. 1–20). New York: Brunner/Mazel.

Figley, C. (1995b). *Compassion fatigue: Coping with secondary traumatic stress disorder in those who treat the traumatized.* New York: Brunner/Mazel.

Fontes , L. (1995). Sharevision: Collaborative supervision and self-care strategies for working with trauma. *The Family Journal: Counseling and Therapy for Couples and Families, 3,* 249–254.

Fox, L. (1987). Teachers or taunters: The dilemma of true discipline for direct care workers with children. *Journal of Child and Youth Care, 3,* 29–54.

Framo, J. (1985). Rationale and techniques of intensive family therapy. In I. Boszormenyi-Nagy & J. L. Framo (Eds.), *Intensive family therapy* (pp. 143–212). New York: Brunner/Mazel.

Franklin, C., & Nurius, P. (1998). *Constructivism in practice: Methods and Challenges.* Milwaukee, WI: Families International.

Freudenberger, H. (1974). Staff burnout. *Journal of Social Issues, 30,* 159–165.

Friesen, V., & Casella, N. (1982). The rescuing therapist: A duplication of the pathogenic family system. *American Journal of Family Therapy, 10,* 57–61.

Fuhrmann, B. (1978). Self-evaluation: An approach for training counselors. *Counselor Education and Supervision, 17,* 315–317.

Gibbs, L., & Gambrill, E. (1999). *Critical thinking for social workers: Exercises for the helping profession* (rev. ed.). Thousand Oaks, CA: Pine Forge Press.

Gibson, R., & Mitchell, M. (1999). *Introduction to counseling and guidance* (5th ed.). Upper Saddle River, NJ: Prentice Hall.

Goldberger, L., & Breznitz, S. (Eds.). (1993). *Handbook of stress: Theoretical and clinical aspects* (2nd ed.). New York: Free Press.

Goodman, J. (1984). Reflection and teacher education: A case study and theoretical analysis. *Interchange, 15,* 9–26.

Goolishian, H., & Winderman, L. (1988). Constructivism, autopoiesis and problem determined systems. *The Irish Journal of Psychotherapy, 9,* 130–143.

Green, J. (1999). *Cultural awareness in the human services: A multi-ethnic approach* (3rd ed.). Needham Heights, MA: Allyn and Bacon.

Grosch, W., & Olsen, D. (1994). *When helping starts to hurt: A new look at burnout among psychotherapists.* New York: Norton.

Haber, R. (1996). *Dimensions of psychotherapy supervision: Maps and means.* New York: Norton.

Hackney, H., & Cormier, S. (1996). *The professional counselor: A process guide to helping* (3rd ed.). Needham Heights, MA: Allyn & Bacon.

Haferkamp, C. (1989). Implications of self-monitoring theory for counseling supervision. *Counselor Education and Supervision, 28,* 290–298.

Haley, J. (1976). *Problem solving therapy* (1st ed.). San Francisco: Jossey-Bass.

Haley, J. (1987). *Problem solving therapy* (2nd ed.). San Francisco: Jossey-Bass.

Haley, J. (1996). *Learning and teaching therapy.* New York: Guilford.

Hansen, J., Stevic, R., & Warner, R. (1977). *Counseling: Theory and process* (2nd ed.). Boston: Allyn & Bacon.

Harris, H., & Maloney, D. (Eds.). (1996). *Human services: Contemporary issues and trends.* Needham Heights, MA: Allyn and Bacon.

Hart, G. (1982). *The process of clinical supervision.* Baltimore, MD: University Park Press.

Hartmann, E. (1997). The concept of boundaries in counselling and psychotherapy. *British Journal of Guidance and Counselling, 25,* 147–162.

Hector, M., Elson, S., & Yager, G. (1977). Teaching counseling skills through self-management procedures. *Counselor Education and Supervision, 17,* 12–22.

Henson-Matthews, C., & Marshall, L. (1988). Self-monitoring and intake interviewer's therapeutic orientation. *Professional Psychology: Research and Practice, 19,* 433–435.

Herman, J. (1992). *Trauma and recovery: The aftermath of violence—from domestic abuse to political terror.* New York: Basic Books.

Heyward, C. (1993). *When boundaries betray us: Beyond illusions of what is ethical in therapy.* San Francisco: Harper Collins.

Hickson, J., & Baltimore, M. (1998). Training school counsellors to work with families. *Guidance and Counselling, 13,* 3–9.

Hoffman, L. (1988). A constructivist position for family therapy. *The Irish Journal of Psychology, 9,* 110–129.

Holloway, E. (1995). *Clinical supervision: A systems approach.* Thousand Oaks, CA: Sage.

Holmes, T., & Rahe, R. (1967). The Social Readjustment Rating Scale. *Journal of Psychosomatic Research, 11,* 213–218.

Holroyd, J. (1988). Questionnaire on resources and stress. *Manual for QRS.* New York: Consulting Psychologists Press.

Hoshmand, L. (1994). *Orientation to inquiry in a reflective professional psychology.* Albany, NY: State University of New York Press.

Hoshmand, L., & Polkinghorne, D. (1992). Redefining the science-practice relationship and professional training. *American Psychologist, 47,* 55–66.

Imel, S. (1992). *Reflective practice in adult education.* ERIC Digest No. 122 (EDO-CE-92-122). Columbus, OH: ERIC Clearinghouse on Adult, Career, and Vocational Education.

International Critical Incident Stress Foundation. (2000). Available: http://www.icisf.org/totry.htm

Irving, J., & Williams, O. (1995). Critical thinking and reflective practice in counselling. *British Journal of Guidance and Counselling, 23,* 107–114.

Ivey, A. (1971). *Microcounseling: Innovations in interviewing training* (2nd ed.). Springfield, IL: Charles C. Thomas.

Ixer, G. (1999). There's no such thing as reflection. *British Journal of Social Work, 29,* 513–527.

Janoff-Bulman, R. (1985). The aftermath of victimization: Rebuilding shattered assumptions. In C. R. Figley (ed.), *Trauma and its wake: The study of treatment of post-traumatic stress disorder* (Vol. 1, pp. 15–25). New York: Brunner/Mazel.

Johnson, L. (1995). *Psychotherapy in the age of accountability.* New York: Norton.

Jourard, S. (1964). *The transparent self.* Princeton, NJ: Van Nostrand Reinholt.

Juhnke, G. (1996). Solution-focused supervision: Promoting supervisee skills and confidence through successful solutions. *Counselor Education and Supervision, 36,* 48–57.

Kagan, N. (1980). *Interpersonal process recall: A method of influencing human interaction.* East Lansing, MI: Michigan State University.

Kahn, W. (1976). Self-management: Learning to be our own counselor. *Personnel and Guidance Journal, 55,* 176–180.

Kane, C. (1995). Family-of-origin work for counseling trainees and practitioners. *The Family Journal: Counseling and Therapy for Couples and Families, 3,* 245–248.

Kanner, A., Coyne, J., Schaefer, C., & Lazarus, R. (1981). Comparison of two models of stress measurement: Daily hassles and uplifts versus major life events. *Journal of Behavioral Medicine, 4,* 1–39.

Kaslow, F. (1986). Themes and patterns. In F. Kaslow (Ed.), *Supervision and training: Models, dilemmas, and challenges* (pp. 237–250). New York: Haworth.

Kassis, J., & Matthews, W. (1987). When families and helpers do not want the mirror. *Journal of Systemic and Strategic Therapies, 6,* 33–43.

Keeley, S., Shemberg, K., Cowell, B., & Zinnbauer, B. (1995). Coping with student resistance to critical thinking. *College Teaching, 43,* 140–145.

Keeney, B. (1979). Ecosystemic epistemology: An alternative paradigm for diagnosis. *Family Process, 18,* 117–129.

Keeney, B. (1983). *Aesthetics of change*. New York: Guilford.

Keeney, B., & Sprenkle, D. (1982). Ecosystemic epistemology: Critical implications for the aesthetics and pragmatics of family therapist. *Family Process, 21,* 1–19.

Keller, J., & Protinsky, H. (1984). A self-management model for supervision. *Journal of Marital and Family Therapy, 10,* 281–288.

Kendrick, R., Chandler, P., & Hatcher, W. (1994). Job demands, stressors, and the school counselor. *The School Counselor, 41,* 365–369.

Kennedy, R. (1988). Counsellor renewal: Let's energize. *Guidance and Counselling, 4,* 17–20.

Kerr, M., & Bowen, M. (1988). *Family evaluation*. New York: Norton.

Kottler, J. (1991). *On being a therapist*. San Francisco: Jossey-Bass.

Kottler, J., & Hazler, R. (1997). *What you never learned in graduate school: A survival guide for therapists*. New York: Norton.

Kuehl, B. (1996). The use of genograms with solution-based and narrative therapies. *The Family Journal: Counseling and Therapy for Couples and Families, 4,* 5–11.

Kurpius, D., Baker, R., & Thomas, I. (1977). *Supervision of applied training: A comparative review*. Westport, CT: Greenwood Press.

Kuypers, J., & Trute, B. (1980). The untrapped worker: A pre-condition for effective family practice. In D. S. Freeman (Ed.), *Perspectives on family therapy* (pp. 57–67). Scarborough, ON: Butterworth & Co.

Lammert, M. (1986). Experience as knowing: Utilizing therapist self-awareness. *Social Casework: The Journal of Contemporary Social Work, 67,* 369–376.

Landau-Stanton, J., & Stanton, D. (1986). Family therapy and systems supervision with the "Pick-a-Dali Circus" model. In F. W. Kaslow (Ed.), *Supervision and training: Models, dilemmas and challenges* (pp. 169–181). Binghampton, NY: Haworth.

Langs, R. (1979). *The supervisory experience*. New York: Aronson.

Lawson, D., & Gaushell, H. (1988). Family autobiography: A useful method for enhancing counselor's personal development. *Counselor Education and Supervision, 28,* 162–167.

Lecomte, C., & Bernstein, B. (1978, March). *Development of self-supervision skills among counselor trainees*. Paper presented at the annual meeting of the American Personnel and Guidance Association, Washington, DC.

Leith, W., McNiece, E., & Fusilier, B. (1989). *Handbook of supervision: A cognitive behavioral system*. Boston: College Hill.

Lewis, G. (1989). The use of color-coded genograms in family therapy. *Journal of Marital and Family Therapy, 15,* 169–175.

Lewis, J. (1979). The inward eye: Monitoring the process of psychotherapy. *Journal of Continuing Education in Psychiatry, 40,* 17-26.

Lewis, J. (1991). *Swimming upstream: Teaching and learning psychotherapy in a biological era*. New York: Brunner/Mazel.

Littrell, J., Lee-Borden, N., & Lorenz, J. (1979). A developmental framework for counseling supervision. *Counselor Education and Supervision, 19,* 129–136.

Lowe, R. (2000). Supervising self-supervision: Constructive inquiry and embedded narratives in case consultation. *Journal of Marital and Family Therapy, 26,* 511–521.

Luthman, S., & Kirschenbaum, M. (1974). *The dynamic family: A study in the development of growth within the family, the treatment of family disorders, and the training of family therapists*. San Francisco: Science & Behavior Books.

Lynch, C. (1981). Not getting caught up in the family system. In J. C. Hansen & D. Rosenthal (Eds.), *Strategies and techniques in family therapy* (pp. 259–265). Springfield, IL: Charles C. Thomas.

Mahoney, M. (1991). *Human change processes: The scientific foundations of psychotherapy*. New York: Basic Books.

Marek, L., Sandifer, D., Beach, A., Coward, R., & Protinsky, H. (1994). Supervision without the problem: A model of solution-focused supervision. *Journal of Family Psychotherapy, 5*(2), 57–64.

Marshall, R. (1982). *Resistant interactions: Child, family and psychotherapist.* New York: Human Science Press.

Martin, D., & Gazda, G. (1970). A method of self-reinforcement for counselor education utilizing the measurement of facilitative conditions. *Counselor Education and Supervision, 9,* 87–92.

Maslach, C. (1982). *Burnout: The cost of caring.* Englewood Cliffs, NJ: Prentice Hall.

Maslach, C., & Jackson, S. (1981). *The Maslach Burnout Inventory.* Palo Alto, CA: Consulting Psychologists Press.

Matthews, C., & Marshall, L. (1988). Self-monitoring and intake interviewer's therapeutic orientations. *Professional Psychology: Research and Practice, 19,* 433–435.

McCann, I., & Pearlman, L. (1990). Vicarious traumatization: A framework for understanding the psychological effects of working with victims. *Journal of Traumatic Stress, 3,* 131–149.

McDaniel, S., & Landau-Stanton, J. (1991). Family-of-origin and family therapy skills training: Both-and. *Family Process, 30,* 459–471.

McGoldrick, M., & Gerson, R. (1985). *Genograms in family assessment.* New York: Norton.

McNamara, D. (1990). Research on teachers' thinking: Its contribution to educating student teachers to think critically. *Journal of Education for Teaching, 16,* 147–160.

McNamee, S., & Gergen, K. (Eds.). (1995). *Therapy as social construction.* Thousand Oaks, CA: Sage

Mead, E. (1990). *Effective supervision: A task oriented model for mental health professions.* New York: Brunner/Mazel.

Mead, G. (1962). *Mind, self, and society.* Chicago: University of Chicago Press.

Meyer, R. (1978). Using self-supervision to maintain counseling skills: A review. *Personnel and Guidance Journal, 57,* 95–98.

Miller, S., Duncan, B., & Hubble, M. (1997). *Escape from Babel: Toward a unifying language for psychotherapy practice.* New York: Norton.

Minuchin, S. (1974). *Families and family therapy.* Cambridge, MA: Harvard University Press.

Mitchell, G. (1995). Reflection: The key to breaking with tradition. *Nursing Science Quarterly, 8,* 57.

Mitchell, J. (1994). *Compassion fatigue: The stress of caring too much.* Available from Visionary Productions, Inc., 2809 West 15th Street, Suite 202, Panama City, FL 32401.

Morrissette, P. (1990). Drawing the curtain on family therapy. *Family Therapy, XVII,* 67–73.

Morrissette, P. (1996a). Beginning family therapist and client system conflict: Analysis and reparation. *Journal of Family Psychotherapy, 7,* 1–13

Morrissette, P. (1996b). Recurring critical issues for student therapists. *Canadian Journal of Counselling, 30,* 31–41.

Morrissette, P. (1999). Family therapist self-supervision: Preliminary guidelines. *The Clinical Supervisor, 18,* 165–183.

Morrissette, P., & Bodard, K. (1989). Troubling youth and their troubling ways: A conceptual framework for a working model. *Child and Youth Care Forum, 20,* 365–373.

Munby, H., & Russell, T. (1989). Educating the reflective teacher: An essay review of two books by Donald Schon. *Journal of Curriculum Studies, 21,* 71–80.

Nelson, M., & Neufeldt, S. (1998). The pedagogy of counseling: A critical examination. *Counselor Education and Supervision, 38,* 70–88.

Neufeldt, S. (1997). A social constructivist approach to counseling supervision. In T. Sexton & B. Griffin (Eds.), *Constructivist thinking in counseling practice, research, and training* (pp. 191–210). New York: Teachers College Press.

Neufeldt, S., Iverson, J., & Juntunen, C. (1995). *Supervision strategies for the first practicum.* Alexandria, VA: American Counseling Association.

Neufeldt, S., Karno, M., & Nelson, M. (1996). A qualitative study of expert's conceptualization of supervisee reflectivity. *Journal of Counseling Psychology, 43,* 3–9.

Nichols, M. (1984). *Family therapy: Concepts and methods.* New York: Gardner Press.

Nichols, M. (1987). *Self in the system: Expanding the limits of family therapy.* New York: Brunner/ Mazel.

Nichols, W. (1989, January/February). Interview with Lynn Hoffman, Evolution or Revolution? Therapists change and change and change. *Family Therapy News,* pp. 10–11.

Norcross, J., & Prochaska, J. (1986). Psychotherapists heal thyself – I. The psychological distress and self-change of psychologists, counselors, and laypersons. *Psychotherapy, 23,* 102–114.

O'Hanlon, B., & Wilk, J. (1987). *Shifting contexts: The generation of effective psychotherapy.* New York: Guilford.

Olsen, M., & Dilley, J. (1988). A new look at stress and the school counselor. *The School Counselor, 35,* 194–198.

Orzek, A. (1984). Mentor-mentee match in training programs based on Chickering's vectors of development. In C. Munson (Ed.), *Supervising student internships in human services* (pp. 71–77). New York: Haworth.

Palmer, S. (1981). *Role stress: How to handle everyday tension.* Toronto, ON: Prentice Hall.

Palombo, J. (1987). Spontaneous self-disclosures in psychotherapy. *Clinical Social Work Journal, 15,* 107–120.

Patterson, P., Williams, L., Grauf-Grounds, C., & Chamow, L. (1998). *Essential skills in family therapy: From the first interview to termination.* New York: Guilford.

Paul, R. (1990). *Critical thinking: What every person needs to survive in a rapidly changing world.* Rohnert Park, CA: Center for Critical Thinking and Moral Critique.

Peacock, E., & Wong, P. (1990). The Stress Appraisal Measure (SAM): A multidimensional approach to cognitive appraisal. *Stress Medicine, 6,* 227–236.

Pearlman, L., & MacIan, P. (1995). Vicarious traumatization: An empirical study of the effects of trauma work on trauma therapists. *Professional Psychology: Research and Practice, 26,* 558–565.

Pearlman, L., & Saakvitne, K. (1995). *Trauma and the therapist: Countertransference and vicarious traumatization in psychotherapy with incest survivors.* New York: Norton.

Penn, P. (1982). Circular questioning. *Family Process, 21,* 267–280.

Peterson, M. (1992). *At personal risk: Boundary violations in professional-client relationships.* New York: Norton.

Pines, A. (1993). Burnout. In L. Goldberger & S. Breznitz (Eds.), *Handbook of stress: Theoretical and clinical aspects* (2nd ed., pp. 386–402). New York: Free Press.

Pines, A., & Aronson, E. (1988). *Career burnout: Causes and cures.* New York: Free Press.

Remer, R., & Ferguson, R. (1995). Becoming a secondary survivor of sexual assault. *Journal of Counseling and Development, 73,* 407–413.

Richman, J. (1986). *Family therapy for suicidal people.* New York: Springer.

Rober, P. (1999). The therapist's inner conversation in family therapy practice: Some ideas about the self of the therapist, therapeutic impasse, and the process of reflection. *Family Process, 38,* 209–228.

Robinson, S., & Kinnier, R. (1988). Self-instructional versus traditional training for teaching basic counseling skills. *Counselor Education and Supervision, 28,* 140–145.

Robinson, S., Kurpius, D., & Froehle, T. (1979). Self-generated performance feedback in interviewing training. *Counselor Education and Supervision, 19,* 91–100.

Ross, D. (1989). First steps in developing a reflective approach. *Journal of Teacher Education, 40,* 22–30.

Roth, R. (1989). Preparing the reflective practitioner: Transforming the apprentice through the dialectic. *Journal of Teacher Education, 40,* 31–35.

Saakvitne, K., & Pearlman, L. (1996). *Transforming the pain: A workbook on vicarious traumatization for helping professionals who work with traumatized clients.* New York: Norton.

Sarason, S. (1977). *Work, aging, and social change.* New York: Free Press.

Satir, V. (1987). The therapist story. In M. Baldwin & V. Satir (Eds.), *The use of self in therapy* (pp. 17–25). New York: Haworth.

Schaufeli, W., Maslach, C., & Marek, T. (Eds.). (1993). *Professional burnout: Recent developments in theory and practice.* Washington, DC: Taylor & Francis.

Schmidt, J., & Davidson, M. (1983). Helping students think. *Personnel and Guidance Journal, 61,* 563–569.

Schon, D. (1983). *The reflective practitioner: How professionals think in action.* New York: Basic Books.

Schwartz, R. (1995). *Internal family systems therapy.* New York: Guilford.

Scott, M., & Stradling, S. (1994). *Counseling for post-traumatic stress disorder.* London: Sage.

Sexton, T., & Griffin, B. (Eds.). (1997). *Constructivist thinking in counseling practice, research, and training.* New York: Teachers College Press.

Shapiro, S., & Reiff, J. (1993). A framework for reflective inquiry on practice: Beyond intuition and experience. *Psychological Reports, 73,* 1379-1394.

Simon, J. (1990). Criteria for therapist self-disclosure. In G. Stricker & M. Fisher (Eds.), *Self-disclosure in the therapeutic relationship* (pp. 207–225). New York: Plenum.

Snyder, M. (1979). Self-monitoring processes. In L. Berkowitz (Ed.), *Advances in experimental social psychology* (Vol. 12, pp. 85–128). New York: Academic Press.

Sowa, C., May, K., & Niles, S. (1994). Occupational stress within the counseling profession: Implication for counselor training. *Counselor Education and Supervision, 34,* 19–29.

Sproul, M., & Gallagher, R. (1982). The genogram as an aid to crisis intervention. *The Journal of Family Practice, 14,* 959–960.

Stamm, B. (1999). *Secondary traumatic stress: Self-care issues for clinicians, researchers, and educators* (2nd ed.). Lutherville, MD: Sidran Press.

Stanton, D. (1992). The time line and the "why now?" question: A technique and rationale for therapy, training, organizational consultation and research. *Journal of Marital and Family Therapy, 18,* 331-343.

Steiden, D. (1993). Self-supervision using discourse analysis. *Supervision Bulletin, VI,* 2.

Steier, F. (Ed.). (1991). *Research and reflexivity.* Thousand Oaks, CA: Sage.

Stickel, S., & Trimmel, K. (1994). Knowing in action: First year counselor's process of reflection. *Elementary School Guidance and Counseling, 29,* 102–109.

Stoltenberg, C., & Delworth, U. (1987). *Supervising counselors and therapists: A developmental model.* San Francisco: Jossey-Bass.

Storm, C. (1995a). Positive self-monitoring: Positive images lead to positive actions. *The Supervision Bulletin, VIII,* 1.

Storm, C. (1995b). Solution-focused ideas guide supervision: An interview with Eve Lipchik. *Supervision Bulletin, VIII,* 2–5.

Storm, C., & Heath, A. (1991). Problem-focused supervision: Rationale, Exemplification, and limitations. *Journal of Family Psychotherapy, 2,* 55–70.

Stoyva, J., & Carlson, J. (1993). A coping/rest model of relaxation and stress management. In L. Goldberger & S. Breznitz (Eds.), *Handbook of stress: Theoretical and clinical aspects* (pp. 724–756). New York: Free Press.

Strean, H. (1990). *Resolving resistances in psychotherapy.* New York: Brunner/Mazel.

Strean, H. (1993). *Therapists who have sex with their patients. Treatment and recovery.* New York: Brunner/Mazel.

Sweitzer, F. (1996). Burnout: Avoiding the trap. In H. Harris & D. Maloney (Eds.), *Human Services: Contemporary issues and trends* (pp. 215–229). Boston: Allyn and Bacon.

Symth, J. (1989). Developing and sustaining critical reflection in teacher education. *Journal of Teacher Education, 40,* 2–9.

Tentoni, S. (1995). The mentoring of counseling students: A concept in search of paradigm. *Counselor Education and Supervision, 35,* 32–42.

Teyber, E. (1992). *Interpersonal process in psychotherapy: A guide for clinical training* (2nd ed.). Pacific Grove, CA: Brooks/Cole.

Thomas, F. (1994). Solution-oriented supervision: The coaxing of expertise. *The Family Journal: Counseling and Therapy for Couples and Families, 2,* 11–18.

Thorenson, R., Miller, M., & Krauskopf, C. (1989). The distressed psychologist: Prevalence and treatment considerations. *Professional Psychology: Research and Practice, 20,* 153–158.

Thorne, B, & Dryden, W. (1991). Keys issues in the training of counselors. In In W. Dryden & B. Thorne (Eds.), *Training and supervision for counseling in action.* London: Sage.

Tiedeman, D. (1979). Letter. *Personnel & Guidance Journal, 56,* 15–16.

Titelman, P. (1992). *The therapist's own family: Toward a differentiation of self.* New York: Aronson.

Todd, T. (1992). Self-supervision: A goal for all supervisors? *Supervision Bulletin, 5,* 3.

Todd, T. (1997a). Purposive systemic supervision models. In T. C. Todd & C. L. Storm (Eds.), *The complete systemic supervisors: Context, philosophy and pragmatics* (pp. 173–194). Needham Heights, MA: Allyn & Bacon.

Todd, T. (1997b). Self-supervision as a universal supervisory goal. In T. C. Todd & C. L. Storm (Eds.), *The complete systemic supervisor: Context, philosophy and pragmatics* (pp. 17–25). Needham Heights, MA: Allyn & Bacon.

Tomm, K., & Wright, L. (1979). Training in family therapy: Perceptual, conceptual, and perceptual skills. *Family Process, 18,* 227–250.

Valent, P. (1995). Survival strategies: A framework for understanding secondary traumatic stress and coping in helpers. In C. Figley (Ed.), *Compassion fatigue: Coping with secondary traumatic stress disorder in those who treat the traumatized* (pp. 21–50). New York: Brunner/Mazel.

van Merrienboer, J., Jelsma, O., & Paas, F. (1992). Training for reflective expertise: A four-component instructional design model for complex cognitive skills. *Educational Technology Research and Development, 40,* 23–43.

Volpe, J. (2000). Traumatic stress: An overview. [Electronic version]. *Trauma Response.*

Wachtel, P. (Ed.). (1982). *Resistance: Psychodynamic and behavioral approaches.* New York: Plenum Press.

Ward, C., & House, R. (1998). Counseling supervision: A reflective model. *Counselor Education and Supervision, 38,* 23–33.

Warnath, C. (1979). Counselor burnout: Existential crisis or a problem for the profession? *Personnel and Guidance Journal, 57,* 325–331.

Warnath, C., & Shelton, J. (1976). The ultimate disappointment: The burned out counselor. *Personnel and Guidance Journal, 55,* 172–175.

Watzlawick, P., Weakland, J., & Fisch, R. (1974). *Change: Principles of problem formulation and problem resolution.* New York: Norton.

Webb, S. (1997). Training for maintaining appropriate boundaries in counselling. *British Journal of Guidance and Counselling, 25,* 175–188.

Wetchler, J. (1990). Solution-focused supervision. *Family Therapy, XVII,* 129–138.

White, M. (1990). *Narrative means to therapeutic ends.* New York: Norton.

White, P., & Franzoni, J. (1990). A multidimensional analysis of the mental health of graduate counselors in training. *Counselor Education and Supervision, 29,* 258–267.

Wiggins Frame, M., & Stevens-Smith, P. (1995). Out of harms way: Enhancing monitoring and dismissal processes in counselor education programs. *Counselor Education and Supervision, 35,* 118–129.

Williams, A. (1995). *Visual and active supervision: Roles, focus, and technique.* New York: Norton.

Williams, M., & Sommer, J. (1994). *Handbook of post-traumatic therapy*. Westport, CT: Greenwood Press.

Wilson, J. (1994). The need for an integrative theory of post-traumatic stress disorder. In M. Williams & J. Sommer (Eds.), *Handbook of post-traumatic therapy* (pp. 3–18). Westport, CT: Greenwood Press.

Winer, J., & Klamen, D. (1997). Psychotherapy supervision: A current method. *Academic Psychiatry, 21*, 141–147.

Winslade, J., Monk, G., & Drewery, W. (1997). Sharpening the critical edge: A social constructionist approach in counselor education. In T. Sexton & B. Griffin (Eds.), *Constructivist thinking in counseling practice, research, and training* (pp. 228–245). New York: Teachers College Press.

Woulff, N., & Bross, A. (1982). *A glass menagerie: Strategies of live supervision*. Unpublished manuscript.

Yager, G. (1987, April). *Self-supervision: What to do when you're stuck without an assigned supervisor*. Paper presented at the Annual Meeting of the American Association for Counseling and Development, New Orleans, LA.

Yager, G., & Park, W. (1986). Counselor self-supervision. *Journal of Counseling and Human Service Professions, 1*, 6–17.

Yassen, J. (1995). Preventing secondary traumatic stress disorder. In C. Figley (Ed.), *Compassion fatigue: Coping with secondary traumatic stress disorder in those who treat the traumatized* (pp. 178–208). New York: Brunner/Mazel.

Zupan, L., Babcock, N., & Morrissette, P. (1988). Therapist centrality in family treatment. *American Journal of Family Therapy, 16*, 319–327.

INDEX